Juan Rodulfo

TikTok Heroes In my Algorithm

First published by Aussie Trading LLC
Copyright © 2025 by Juan Rodulfo
All rights reserved.

No part of this publication may be reproduced, stored, or transmitted in any form or by any means, electronic, mechanical, photocopying, recording, scanning or otherwise without written permission from the publisher. It is illegal to copy this book, publish it on a website, or distribute it by any other means without permission.

Juan Rodulfo has no responsibility for the persistence or accuracy of URLs of external or third-party Internet websites referenced in this publication and does not warrant that the content of such websites is, or will remain, accurate or appropriate.

The names used by companies to distinguish their products are often claimed as trademarks. All trademarks and product names used in this book and on its cover, trade names, service marks, trademarks are trademarks of their respective owners. The publishers and the book are not associated with any products or suppliers mentioned in this book. None of the companies or organizations referenced in the book have endorsed it.

Library of Congress Catalog
Names: Rodulfo, Juan
ISBN: 978-1-08810788-1 (paperback)
ISBN: 978-1-08797532-0 (e-book)
ISBN: 979-8-3306-5773-5 (hardcover)
First edition
Layout by Juan Rodulfo
Cover art by Guaripete Solutions
Production: Aussie Trading, LLC
books@aussietrading.ltd
Printed in the USA

juanrodulfo.com

juanrodulfo.com

> You must be the change you wish to see in the world.
> **Gandhi**

juanrodulfo.com

Preface

Been a hero does not mean to wear a cap, or have superpowers, been a hero is as simply as risk your own comfort to help those in need, by any mean, no matter if "their actual issue" directly or indirectly affects your status.

These TikTok heroes, are regular humans whom from their own places, home, office, car, backyard, and just facing their camera phones, with no scripts, no filters, no post editions, no power strings attached, decided to rise their voices against the tyranny and become amplifiers and clear channels of fact checked information addressed to those who spent most of the time on social media. As the circles of power want society to be, a society with no formal education, ignorant, dissociated from reality and divided, so they can keep parasitically enriching from national treasures.

A new concept has been released to denominate these social media actors: Content Creators, which is someone who produces and shares various forms of content, including written articles, videos, images, and audio, for online platforms, often with the goal of entertaining, educating, or connecting with an audience.

There is a cup in evolution from within the White House, and Nazi signs has been flagrantly and purposedly exposed by members or people associated with Donald Trump and his cabinet, Human Rights are being violated daily, and Federal Judges orders mocked.

I along with more than eight million Venezuelans flee the Nicolas Maduro dictatorship, seeking refugee in this country, where democracy is still a thing, and people of all nations can share the same soil, (hope not to refer to it in past tense).

In my book Manual for Gorillas: 9 Rules to be the "*fer-pect*" Dictator, I published a 2018 study by the Bertelsmann Stiftung which concluded that a billion more people live under dictatorship now than was the case 15 years ago. The findings were the sum of research for the Bertelsmann Stiftung's "Transformation Index" in which the institute analyzed the quality of democracy, the market economy and leadership in 129 countries. While the researchers concluded that the number of people living in democracies rose from four billion to 4.2 billion between 2003 and 2017, they also found that 3.3 billion people lived under dictatorship last year compared to 2.3 billion in 2003. The report further warned that growing restrictions on citizens' rights and legal standards were an acute problem in democracies.[i]

Our civilization has lost the interest for the books, induced of course by politics designed with that goal and pushed by the circles of power that control human population, but since we cannot find the majority of the voters at libraries and university campuses, to save democracy we must go to the place where they are: social media.

Even though some rules of TikTok are "strict", the algorithm works a bit more freely than the "algorithm" of Meta (Facebook), Twitter ("x"), Instagram=Facebook, and others, in fact, I found myself on my few spare time when want to see mild content, life is life, everything is awesome, I go to IG (Instagram), and when want to check the latest HR Violations, Dictatorship Movements of the actual government of the US, I go to TikTok, where content creators have more time to fully express their ideas, are not constantly blocked by the algorithm and reach all those who are sick of Zuckerberg/Musk biased platforms.

Create something needs time, time is money, and to create this content, they must set aside their own interests to research, read, analyze, compare, set the scene, etc., some of them mentioned in this book, have teams which help them in the process, adding subtitles, scenarios, references and other marketing tools, other segment of these content creators, involved in the defense of democracy are Government Officials, who believe in their roles as temporary holders of a power that belongs to the people as a whole, are not afraid to lose their bureaucratic seats, are not oligarchy puppets and has not forgotten we have only one planet for all and the last segment are those whose content is not directly oriented to dismantle the coup de tat in evolution, but to shed light to those supporters of the actual regime, who still believe earth is flat and supernatural powers are checking us from the sky, like Neil deGrasse Tyson, Reid Moon, Roy Casagrande, Jared Van, Brandt Robinson, @alberta.nyc, @alimcforever and hundreds more, outside my algorithm.

Special mention to Claudia Sheinbaum Pardo, current President of Mexico, whose social media presence is a crystal image of her human persona, real and simple, as we human really are, without filters, real smiles, heart warmed speech, no rush in her words, a remembrance of Barack Obama…, she has successfully assumed the -non included in her duties as Mexico's president- task of educate and dismantle the lies and attacks of the actual occupant of the white house.

This book compiles the profiles of those who the algorithm has kept in my TikTok feed, for the last months of 2024 and first trimester of 2025, as an exaltation to their self-sacrificing labor shedding light on the stuff the wanna be neo-Nazi dictator, would like to hold hiding from scrutiny.

If TikTok unilaterally decides or the dictatorship succeeds and gets them banned, I want to maintain published records of their

juanrodulfo.com

achievements in pro of democracy and the education of those who refuse to read books, or just simply find themselves in search of current information and knowledge like me.

juanrodulfo.com

Aaron Gideon Parnas
@aaronparnas1

Aaron Gideon Parnas (b. 1999) is an American lawyer and democratic activist. Parnas is the son of Lev Parnas, known for his role in the Trump-administration Trump–Ukraine scandal. Parnas, who was once a staunch Republican and supporter of President Donald Trump, has since become an activist in support of the Democratic Party.

During the 2022 Russian invasion of Ukraine, Parnas became a pro-Ukrainian TikToker. Parnas works as a securities litigation attorney at a law firm in Washington, D.C.

Aaron Parnas is the son of Lev Parnas and Barbara Ison. Parnas' father was a close confidante of former New York City Mayor Rudy Giuliani and was convicted and charged for his role in the Trump-Ukraine scandal. Parnas is of Jewish-Ukrainian descent. In 2017, at the age of eighteen, Parnas completed both a diploma from Florida Atlantic University High School and a B.A. in political science and criminal justice at Florida Atlantic University. Despite not being old enough to vote, he campaigned door-to-door for Marco Rubio and Donald Trump.

He graduated from George Washington University Law School, with honors, in 2020 at the age of twenty-one. While in law school, Aaron won multiple awards for his oral advocacy skills including the Cohen & Cohen Mock Trial Award, and the Graduation Award for Excellence in Pre-Trial and Trial Advocacy. In 2019, Parnas worked as a summer intern at Greenberg Traurig, the former law firm of Giuliani. Prior to joining his employer (law firm), Aaron served as a law clerk at the United States District Court for the Middle District of Florida.

In 2020, Parnas published a memoir titled Trump First: How the President and His Associates Turned Their Backs on Me and My Family. This followed Parnas' father being implicated in a variety of criminal activities, in 2019, including involvement in illegal campaign fundraising and working to pressure the Ukrainian government into opening investigations into potential opponents of Trump. Parnas voted for and campaigned for Joe Biden in 2020. Parnas works at a Washington, D.C. based law firm. He is also a

Democratic digital strategist. In early 2021, Parnas began serving as the press secretary for the Miami-Dade Democratic Party.

In a February 24, 2022, interview, Parnas began posting TikTok videos expressing shock about the 2022 Russian invasion of Ukraine and published information about his relatives that were trying to evacuate Ukraine. Parnas's TikTok saw success and he became notable as a pro-Ukrainian TikToker. He has amassed more than three million followers on TikTok. He was one of several influencers to speak with President Joe Biden to combat disinformation about the Russian invasion of Ukraine.[ii]

juanrodulfo.com

ACLU @ACLU

In the years following World War I, America was gripped by the fear that the Communist Revolution that had taken place in Russia would spread to the United States. As is often the case when fear outweighs rational debate, civil liberties paid the price. In November 1919 and January 1920, in what notoriously became known as the "Palmer Raids," Attorney General Mitchell Palmer began rounding up and deporting so-called radicals. Thousands of people were arrested without warrants and without regard to constitutional protections against unlawful search and seizure. Those arrested were brutally treated and held in horrible conditions.

In the face of these egregious civil liberties abuses, a small group of people decided to take a stand and thus was born the American Civil Liberties Union.

The ACLU has evolved in the years since from this small group of idealists into the nation's premier defender of the rights enshrined in the U.S. Constitution. With more than 1.1 million members, 500 staff attorneys, thousands of volunteer attorneys, and offices throughout the nation, the ACLU of today continues to fight government abuse and to vigorously defend individual freedoms including speech and religion, a woman's right to choose, the right to due process, citizens' rights to privacy and much more. The ACLU stands up for these rights even when the cause is unpopular, and sometimes when nobody else will. While not always in agreement with us on every issue, Americans have come to count on the ACLU for its unyielding dedication to principle. The ACLU has become so ingrained in American society that it is hard to imagine an America without it.

One of the ACLU's earliest battles was the Scopes Trial of 1925. When the state of Tennessee passed a law banning the teaching of evolution, the ACLU recruited biology teacher John T. Scopes to challenge the law by teaching the banned subject in his class. When Scopes was eventually prosecuted, the ACLU partnered with celebrated attorney Clarence Darrow to defend him. Although Scopes was found guilty (the verdict was later overturned because of a sentencing error), the trial made national headlines and helped persuade the public on the importance of academic freedom.

After the Japanese attack on Pearl Harbor, President Franklin Roosevelt ordered all people of Japanese descent, most of whom were

American citizens, be sent to "war relocation camps." Eventually more than 110,000 Japanese Americans were sent to these internment camps. The ACLU, led by its California affiliates, stood alone in speaking out about this atrocity.

In 1954, the ACLU joined forces with the NAACP to challenge racial segregation in public schools. The resulting Supreme Court decision in Brown v. Board of Education that ended the era of "separate but equal" was a major victory for racial justice.

The ACLU was also involved in 1973 in the Supreme Court victories in Roe v. Wade and Doe v. Bolton, which held that the right to privacy encompasses a woman's right to decide whether she will terminate or continue a pregnancy 2003, the ACLU helped persuade the Supreme Court in Lawrence v. Texas to expand upon the privacy rights established in Roe when it struck down a Texas law making sexual intimacy between same-sex couples a crime.

One of the most noted moments in the ACLU's history occurred in 1978 when the ACLU defended a Nazi group that wanted to rally through the Chicago suburb of Skokie, Illinois, where many Holocaust survivors lived. The ACLU persuaded a federal court to strike down three ordinances that placed significant restrictions on the Nazis' First Amendment right to march and express their views. The decision to take the case was a demonstration of ACLU's commitment to the principle that constitutional rights must apply to even the most unpopular groups if they are going to be preserved for everyone. Many now consider this one of the ACLU's finest hours.

That commitment to principles in demanding situations continues today. Since the tragic terrorist attacks of 9/11, the ACLU has been working vigorously to oppose policies that sacrifice our fundamental freedoms in the name of national security. From opposing the Patriot Act to challenging warrantless spying to challenging the indefinite detention of terrorism suspects without charge or trial, the ACLU is committed to restoring fundamental freedoms lost as a result of policies that expand the government's power to invade privacy, imprison people without due process and punish dissent.

The ACLU also remains a champion of segments of the population who have traditionally been denied their rights, with much of our work today focused on equality for people of color, women, gay and transgender people, prisoners, immigrants, and people with disabilities.

Back in 1920, the individual freedoms enumerated in the Constitution had never been fully tested in the courts, making them largely meaningless for ordinary people. Since then, principles of individual freedom, protection against arbitrary government action, freedom of religion, freedom of speech and press, due process of law, equal protection, and privacy have become codified in our laws and their protections widely enforced. The advancement of civil rights and social justice over the past century represents one of the most significant developments in American history, and the ACLU has been integral to this process.

But the work of defending freedom never ends, and in our vibrant and passionate society, difficult struggles over individual rights and liberties are not likely to disappear anytime soon. The ACLU is committed to fighting for freedom and the protection of constitutional rights for generations to come.

The ACLU dares to create a more perfect union — beyond one person, party, or side. Our mission is to realize this promise of the United States Constitution for all and expand the reach of its guarantees.

We have grown from that roomful of civil libertarians to more than 1.7 million members. The ACLU today is the nation's largest public interest law firm, with a 50-state network of staffed, autonomous affiliate offices. We appear before the United States Supreme Court more than any other organization except the U.S. Department of Justice. About 100 ACLU staff attorneys collaborate with about 2,000 volunteer attorneys in handling close to 2,000 cases annually.

The ACLU is non-profit and non-partisan. We do not receive any government funding. Member dues and contributions and grants from private foundations and individuals pay for the work we do. The ACLU, with headquarters in New York City, litigates across the nation and all the way to the U.S. Supreme Court. Our Washington, D.C., legislative office lobbies the U.S. Congress. We use strategic communications to educate the public about issues. And the ACLU has expanded its reach by applying international human rights standards in our complex Post 9/11 world. A number of national projects address specific civil liberties issues: AIDS, capital punishment, lesbian and gay rights, immigrants' rights, prisoners' rights, reproductive freedom, voting rights, women's rights, and workplace rights.

If you believe your civil liberties have been violated, or if you wish to join the ACLU, contact your local ACLU affiliate from the listing in the telephone directory, or write to the national headquarters, Attention: Membership Department. Briefing papers, each on a different civil liberties issue, and other publications and information are available from the Communications Department of the ACLU's national office in New York.[iii]

National Office:
American Civil Liberties Union

125 Broad Street, 18th Floor.
New York, NY 10004-2400
(212) 549-2500
E-mail: infoaclu@aclu.org

William Tong @agwilliamtong

William Tong is the 25th Attorney General to serve Connecticut since the office was established by the state constitution in 1897. He first took office in 2019 and is currently serving his second term.

Attorney General Tong is a national leader in many of the most consequential lawsuits and investigations in our country today, including bipartisan, multistate efforts to hold the addiction industry accountable for their role in the opioid crisis; to restore fair competition and prices in the generic drug industry; to hold social media giants accountable for the harms they may cause to kids and young people; to stop robocall scammers; and to ensure corporations safeguard our personal information from misuse and respect consumers' rights regarding the collection and use of their information.

As a father and the son of immigrant small business owners, Attorney General Tong knows first-hand how Connecticut families are squeezed by rising costs that are unaffordable and unsustainable, and he has prioritized efforts to drive down energy costs, expand access to reliable broadband internet, and ensure access to affordable healthcare.

Attorney General Tong works every day to safeguard our civil rights and freedoms, fighting alongside state attorneys general nationwide to protect the rights of women, minority communities, immigrants, and the LGBTQ+ community. He has vowed to fight in any court, in any state, anywhere access to reproductive healthcare is under threat. He is aggressively defending Connecticut's post- Sandy Hook gun laws against challenges by out of state gun lobbies. Under his leadership, Connecticut has sued ExxonMobil to end its ongoing, systematic campaign of lies around fossil fuels and climate change.

Under Attorney General Tong's leadership, Connecticut resolved two of the most challenging, longest running state lawsuits – committing to historic investments in educational opportunities for Hartford students to end more than 30 years of litigation and court oversight in the Sheff v. O'Neill case, and ending court oversight of the Department of Children and Families following documented, significant improvement on behalf of our state's most vulnerable children.

Attorney General Tong currently serves as Eastern Region Chair and Finance Chair of the National Association of Attorneys General. He also serves on the Executive Committee of the Democratic Attorneys General Association.

Attorney General Tong previously practiced for 18 years as a litigator in both state and federal courts, first at Simpson Thacher & Bartlett LLP in New York City and then at Finn Dixon & Herling LLP in Stamford. He served for 12 years as a State Representative in the Connecticut General Assembly, where he served as House Chair of the Judiciary Committee as well as the Banking Committee. In 2006, he became the first Asian American elected to any state office in Connecticut history.

During his service in the legislature, Attorney General Tong was the author and driver of several major Connecticut laws, helping lead the state's efforts against gun violence and domestic violence, among many other critical laws and initiatives.

A Connecticut native, Attorney General Tong grew up in the Hartford area and attended schools in West Hartford. He graduated from Phillips Academy Andover, Brown University, and the University of Chicago Law School.

Tong is the oldest of five children and grew up working side-by-side with his immigrant parents in their family's Chinese restaurant. He and his wife, Elizabeth, live in Stamford with their three children and way too many pets. Elizabeth is the Senior Vice President at L'Oreal USA. In quieter moments, General Tong likes to fly fish (and tie flies), try all the great foods and restaurants across Connecticut and is an amateur carpenter and cook.

He is the first Asian American elected to any state office in Connecticut history, and the first Chinese American to be elected Attorney General nationwide.[iv]

Alberta Tech @alberta.nyc

This is the only information I was able to find on the web about her:

MERCH!
alberta.nyc

Instagram
instagram.com/alberta.tech

TikTok
tiktok.com/@alberta.nyc

Everything else!
beacons.ai/albertatech

@ALIMCFOREVER

This is the only information I was able to find on the web about her:

Understand History. See Through the Bullsh*t.

History is not neutral. It is shaped by power, rewritten by winners, and weaponized in ways most people do not even notice.

No one is coming to save us. Corporations, governments, and banks serve their own interests first.

Real change happens when we take back control—over knowledge, resources, and communities.

More links: https://alimcforever.com

Alexandria Ocasio-Cortez @aoc

Born in the Parkchester neighborhood of The Bronx, Alexandria's parents moved the family 30 minutes north to Yorktown in search of a stronger public school for her and her brother. Alexandria's mother was born and raised in Puerto Rico and worked throughout her childhood as a domestic worker. Alexandria's father was a second-generation Bronxite, who ran a small business in The Bronx. Throughout her childhood, Representative Ocasio-Cortez traveled regularly to The Bronx to spend time with her extended family. From an early age, the stark contrast in educational opportunities available to her and her cousins, based on their respective zip codes, made an impression on her.

After high school, Alexandria attended Boston University and graduated with degrees in Economics and International Relations (and tens of thousands of dollars in student loans).

During this period, she also had the opportunity to intern in the office of the late Senator Ted Kennedy. Her role in Senator Kennedy's office provided a firsthand view of the heartbreak families endured after being separated by ICE. These experiences led the Congresswoman to organize Latinx youth in The Bronx and across the United States, eventually, she began work as an Educational Director with the National Hispanic Institute, a role in which she helped Americans, DREAMers and undocumented youth in community leadership and college readiness.

Following the financial crisis of 2008, tragedy struck when her father passed away suddenly from cancer. The medical bills and other growing expenses placed their home at risk of foreclosure. Alexandria pulled extra shifts to work as a waitress and bartender to support her family, deepening her commitment to issues impacting working-class people.

First Political Campaign

During the 2016 presidential election, Alexandria worked as a volunteer organizer for Bernie Sanders in the South Bronx, expanding her skills in electoral organizing and activism.

Shortly thereafter, she was inspired by demonstrations being led by Indigenous communities at Standing Rock, South Dakota in opposition to a new pipeline. She decided to travel across the country to join them, and left the experience resolved to dedicate her life to public service. A few months later, she launched her first campaign for Congress.

"The campaign was a long shot from the start. 'Everyone said, 'She's really cute, but maybe next time,'" Ocasio-Cortez recalls. Crowley, the fourth-ranking House Democrat, was a prolific fundraiser who had been in Congress since 1999. Her campaign was mostly volunteers. Staffers wrote their job titles on Post-it notes above their desks in their small Queens office. Ever the activist, her campaign had an informal, flexible structure resembling "leaderless" social movements like the one she saw at Standing Rock." – Time magazine, March 21, 2019

In June 2018, Alexandria's campaign shocked the political establishment, when she defeated incumbent Joe Crowley. Her campaign was driven entirely by grassroots volunteers and donations. The Congresswoman refused to take any contributions from corporations, a practice she continues to this day.

First Term

In January of 2019, Congresswoman Ocasio-Cortez was sworn-in as the youngest woman and youngest Latina ever to serve in Congress. Her first piece of legislation was the Green New Deal resolution, which envisions a 10-year national mobilization, akin to FDR's New Deal, that would put millions to work in good-paying, union jobs repairing the nation's infrastructure, reducing air and water pollution, and fighting the intertwined economic, social, racial and climate crises crippling the country.

Over her first term, she introduced a total of twenty-three pieces of legislation. Among them is her Loan Shark Prevention Act, which would cap credit card interest rates at 15%. The Congresswoman also introduced a group of bills collectively titled 'Just Society,' which would raise the federal poverty line, include immigrants in social safety net programs, require federal contractors to pay a living wage, strengthen renters' rights, and decrease recidivism.

In her first term, the Congresswoman saw three amendments pass into law, despite Republican control of the Senate and Presidency. One shifted $5 million from the failed war on drugs to treatment for opioid addiction and another secured $10 million to clean up toxic bombardment sites in Puerto Rico. Most notably, the Congresswoman also worked with Senator Schumer to include a Funeral Assistance Program into the COVID-19 relief package. To date, the program has reimbursed over a billion in funeral expenses to Americans who lost loved ones to COVID-19.

"There are some politicians who are particularly good on policy, and there are some politicians who are good communicators, and there are some politicians that have a way about them that relates very well to ordinary people. Alexandria has all three of those characteristics." – Senator Bernie Sanders

The Congresswoman also quickly gained a reputation as an effective questioner in committee hearings. Through committee hearings, she pressured a major pharmaceutical company into lowering the price of a drug that reduces HIV transmission; forced a defense contractor to return $16.1 million in federal funding; and got Michael Cohen to state on the record that President Donald Trump was engaging in tax fraud and to divulge other information that helped the New York Attorney General open an investigation into the Trump Organization.

The Congresswoman also maintained a commitment to doing a town hall nearly every month of her first term, hosting a total of twenty-five town halls, all of which provided language translation services and accessibility for the hearing impaired. The District Office also opened cases for 1,400 constituents, assisting with everything from immigration visas and Social Security payments to small business loans and veteran's benefits. Various institutions in NY-14 also received $470M in federal grants during our first term.

Second Term

In January 2021, Rep. AOC was sworn in for her second term in Congress. Just a few days later, on January 6, the Capitol was breached for the first time since the War of 1812. Along with several colleagues, Rep. AOC hid in one of the office buildings until the Capitol was secured and the House was called to vote to verify the results of the 2020 presidential election. In the wake of the attacks, the Congresswoman called to expel Members of Congress who had voted to invalidate the elections and who had urged on those domestic terrorists that attacked the Capitol. She also voted for a second time to impeach President Trump.

In March, Congress passed the American Rescue Plan – President Biden's plan to help the nation recover from COVID-19. The Congresswoman and other progressives fought hard to include key provisions, including an expanded Child Tax Credit, which most families began receiving in monthly installments that summer.

"When I ask (Rep. Ayanna) Pressley what popular narratives (about Rep. Ocasio-Cortez) miss, she cites humility. 'She certainly did not set out to be an icon or even a history maker. I think it was her destiny, but there is no calculation.' As Ocasio-Cortez puts it, 'I don't want to be a savior, I want to be a mirror.'" - Vanity Fair, October 28, 2020.

In April 2021, the Congresswoman reintroduced her Green New Deal resolution – growing the list of co-sponsors to over 115. In the three years since the resolution was first introduced, the Green New Deal has inspired over a dozen pieces of legislation and ten regional Green New Deals.

In August 2021, after the federal eviction moratorium expired, Rep. Ocasio-Cortez joined Rep. Cori Bush for a sit-in on the Capitol Steps that lasted several days. Ultimately, the Biden administration reversed its position and extended the ban. Though their executive order was struck down by conservatives on the Supreme Court several weeks later, this time was invaluable for families and landlords trying to access Emergency Rental Relief and stay in their homes.

Later that month, Rep. Ocasio-Cortez worked with the State Department to help Afghan evacuees. Along with Rep. Barbara Lee, Rep. Ocasio-Cortez led 70 Members of Congress in calling on the Biden administration to increase the cap on refugees to 200,000 people.

In September, unprecedented floods devastated the Congresswoman's district and other parts of New York and New Jersey. Sadly, several constituents were killed – having drowned in basement apartments. In the aftermath, the Congresswoman worked with the President and others to get one of the fastest FEMA disaster declarations in history. So far, almost 25,000 New York families have received $165 million in assistance.

By the end of 2021, Rep. Ocasio-Cortez had submitted 30 amendments, including one which doubled the funding to replace and update lead water infrastructure in schools and childcare programs — and another which prohibited funds from being used to provide weapons or military aid or military training to Saudi Arabia's Rapid Intervention Force (RIF), the unit responsible for the murder of U.S. journalist Jamal Khashoggi.

In March of 2022, President Biden signed into law an omnibus bill to keep the federal government funded and open. This legislation included nearly $7 million in funding for ten community projects that will serve New York's 14th Congressional District. The community projects include youth violence interventions, educational support, workforce training in green jobs and home healthcare, and support for Plaza Del Sol Health Center and Elmhurst Hospital.[v]

JOHN ARAVOSIS @ARAVOSIS

aravosis The Aravosis Report

Follow   Message

295 Following   764.7K Followers   46.4M Likes

Trump & Ukraine News
LIVE M-F 6pm ET
Follow me on YouTube: JohnAravosisDC

🔗 linktr.ee/aravosis

John Aravosis is a long-time Washington, DC-based lawyer, reporter, and political consultant. The Aravosis Reporter is a daily show, Monday to Friday, at 6pm ET, focusing on the latest news from Washington, and the war in Ukraine.

More links: https://linktr.ee/aravosis

Ashley Thee Barroness
@ASHLEYTHEEBARRONESS

ashleytheebarroness ashleytheebarroness

Follow Message

6456 Following 90.8K Followers 1.1M Likes

🎥 History & headlines—decoded, unfiltered, and way more interesting than school

🔗 linktr.ee/Ashleytheebarroness

Found on her YouTube channel: Here, we explore world history, Black history, and events shaping our world today. Expect powerful stories, hidden truths, and deep dives into the moments that matter. If you love learning, questioning, and staying informed, you are in the right place.

More links:
https://linktr.ee/Ashleytheebarroness

juanrodulfo.com

@ATHEISTICDEIST

This is the only information I was able to find on the web about him:

More links:
https://www.atom.bio/atheisticdeist

BERNIE SANDERS @BERNIE

Bernie Sanders is serving his fourth term in the U.S. Senate after winning re-election in 2024. His previous 16 years in the House of Representatives make him the longest serving independent member of Congress in American history.

Born in 1941 in Brooklyn, Sanders attended James Madison High School, Brooklyn College, and the University of Chicago. After graduating in 1964, he moved to Vermont. In 1981, he was elected to the first of four terms as mayor of Burlington. Sanders lectured at the John F. Kennedy School of Government at Harvard and at Hamilton College in upstate New York before his 1990 election as Vermont's at-large member in Congress.

The Almanac of American Politics calls Sanders a "practical and successful legislator." Throughout his career he has focused on the shrinking American middle class and the growing income and wealth gaps in the United

States. As chairman of the Senate Committee on Veterans' Affairs, Sanders in 2014 passed legislation reforming the VA health care system. Congressional Quarterly said he was able "to bridge Washington's toxic partisan divide and cut one of the most significant deals in years."

Today, Sanders remains on the veterans committee and serves as the Ranking Member of the Senate Health, Education, Labor, and Pensions (HELP) Committee after he was tapped by Senate leadership to be the chairman last Congress. He also serves on the Environment and Public Works Committee, where he has focused on global warming and rebuilding our nation's crumbling infrastructure. He is a member of the Senate Finance Committee, where he prioritizes protecting Social Security, Medicare, and Medicaid and creating a fair tax system. He also sits on the Senate Budget Committee, which he was previously chairman of, and led the committee's fight against corporate greed.[vi]

Brad Bernstein
@BRADBERNSTEINLAW

With decades of dedication to immigration law, my role as President of Spar & Bernstein has positioned us as a beacon for those navigating the complexities of U.S. immigration policies. We have transformed thousands of individual stories into successful legal outcomes, reflecting our firm's commitment to client-centered advocacy and nuanced legal strategy.

Our team, under my leadership, consistently delivers on the promise of personalized legal solutions, with specialties ranging from work and employment visas, family-based immigration, investor visas, to deportation defense.

More links:
https://linktr.ee/Realbradbernstein

STEWART REYNOLDS @BRITTLESTAR

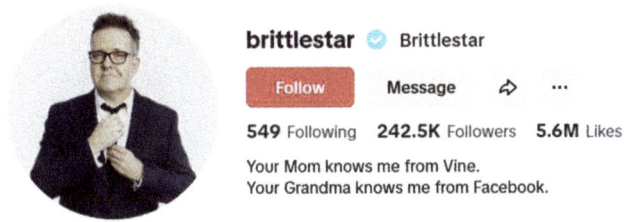

Brittlestar is the stage name of Stewart Reynolds, a Stratford, Ontario based comedian, writer, communications consultant, and online television show host.

His campaign for KFC Canada was the world's most watched branded video on Facebook in the summer of 2017.

Reynolds was born to Scottish immigrants Bette (b. 1947) and Stuart (d. 2024), and is based in Stratford, Ontario. Bette appeared on the 13th season of The Voice UK.

As a comedian, Reynolds brands himself as "the internet's favorite dad. Recurring themes in his work are parodies of Canadian politicians, 1980s nostalgia, and support for public health messages about the COVID-19 pandemic. He uses his influence to support charitable causes including the Christmas Wish Tree program and Women's Crisis Services of Waterloo Region.

Reynolds co-hosts a daily online morning show called The Morning Show Thing with his wife Shannon.

In the Summer of 2017, Reynolds' media campaign for KFC Canada was the global most popular branded video on Facebook.

In April 2022, Reynolds collaborated on comedy videos with Gurdeep Pandher and in December 2022 he released a Christmas music video with actor Emma Rudy Put on Another Christmas Song.[vii]

Captain Mark Kelly
@captmarkkelly

Mark Kelly (born February 21, 1964, Orange, New Jersey, U.S.) is an American astronaut and politician who served in the U.S. Senate (2020–), representing Arizona. He is the identical twin brother of astronaut Scott Kelly.

Mark Kelly received a bachelor's degree in marine engineering and transportation from the United States Merchant Marine Academy at Kings Point, New York, in 1986. Scott and Mark became pilots in the U.S. Navy in 1987 and 1989, respectively. Mark flew thirty-nine combat missions during the Persian Gulf War in 1991. Both brothers graduated from the U.S. Navy Test Pilot School in Patuxent River, Maryland, in 1994. That year Mark also received a master's degree in aeronautical engineering from the U.S. Naval Postgraduate School in Monterey, California.

Mark and Scott Kelly began their astronaut training in August 1996. Mark's first spaceflight was as pilot of the space shuttle Endeavour on the STS-108 mission (December 5–17, 2001), which carried three astronauts and supplies to the International Space Station (ISS). Mark flew again to the ISS in July 2006 on the 13-day STS-121 mission as pilot of the space shuttle Discovery, which carried a German astronaut to the ISS, increasing its crew from two to three. Mark made two subsequent flights to the ISS as mission commander. On the STS-124 mission (May 31–June 14, 2008) of the space shuttle Discovery, commanded by Mark, the Japanese experiment module Kibo was joined to the ISS.

Scott was launched to the ISS on the Russian spacecraft Soyuz TMA-01M on October 8, 2010, and was on board until March 16, 2011. Mark was originally scheduled to arrive at the ISS in February 2011 as commander of the space shuttle Endeavour's last mission, STS-134, which was to attach the Alpha Magnetic Spectrometer, an experiment designed to study antimatter, dark matter, and cosmic rays, to the ISS, and the Kelly twins would then have become the first siblings in space at the same time. However, delays in launching an earlier mission pushed STS-134's launch to May 16, 2011.

Mark's wife, U.S. Rep. Gabrielle Giffords of Arizona, was seriously wounded during an assassination attempt on January 8, 2011. At Mark's request the National Aeronautics and Space Administration (NASA) appointed a backup commander, Rick Sturckow, if Mark would be unable to complete preparing for STS-134. However, Giffords recovered from her injuries much more quickly than expected, and she was able to watch Mark launch into space. STS-134 returned to Earth on June 1, and in October Mark left NASA and the U.S. Navy to help Giffords with her recovery. One month later Giffords and Mark published Gabby: A Story of Courage and Hope (written with Jeffrey Zaslow). In 2013, in response to the Newtown shootings of 2012, they founded Americans for Responsible Solutions, an organization and political action committee dedicated to reducing gun violence in the United States. In 2019 Mark announced that he was running for a U.S. Senate seat from Arizona, and he was elected in November 2020; he took office the following month.[viii]

Claudia Sheinbaum Pardo
@claudiasheinbaum

Claudia Sheinbaum (born June 24, 1962, Mexico City, Mexico) is a Mexican politician and environmental engineer who is the President of Mexico. She is the first woman and the first Jewish person to be elected to the post. Sheinbaum previously served as mayor of Mexico City (2018–23) before stepping down to run in the presidential election in 2024 as a candidate for the National Regeneration Movement (Movimiento Regeneración Nacional; MORENA). She won a landslide victory in June and began her six-year term on October 1.

Sheinbaum is also known for her scientific research and policy advocacy on matters of energy efficiency, sustainability, and the environment. She was one of the scientists and policymakers who shared the 2007 Nobel Prize for Peace for their work on the United Nations

Intergovernmental Panel on Climate Change (IPCC).

Sheinbaum is the second daughter of Annie Pardo Cemo, a biologist and professor emeritus at the National Autonomous University of Mexico (UNAM) in Mexico City, and Carlos Sheinbaum, a chemical engineer. After spending her childhood in Mexico City, Sheinbaum enrolled at UNAM to study physics. For her master's and doctorate degrees (also at UNAM), she studied energy engineering and conducted her doctoral research at Lawrence Berkeley National Laboratory in Berkeley, California, U.S. Her dissertation compared trends in energy consumption in Mexico with those of other industrialized countries. Sheinbaum returned to UNAM as a member of the engineering faculty in 1995.

Sheinbaum was politically active as a student and professor in the 1980s and '90s. Although she helped found the student-led Revolutionary Democratic Party in 1998, she would not hold office until the turn of the 21st century. In 2000 she was appointed Mexico City's environmental minister by Mayor Andrés Manuel López Obrador, with whom she shares strong political ties. In the role, she oversaw the introduction of the city's bus system, Metrobus, and the construction of a second story of the Periférico, a beltway road that encircles Mexico City's urban zone. After López Obrador lost his bid to become Mexico's president in the 2006 election, Sheinbaum returned to UNAM, where she contributed to the climate change mitigation section of the IPCC's fourth and fifth assessment reports (see also global warming policy) and continued her scientific research. The IPCC was awarded a Nobel Peace Prize following the fourth assessment's publication in 2007.

In 2015 Sheinbaum was elected mayor of the Tlalpan district of Mexico City. In this role, she stressed the importance of water rights and fair usage. Although she received criticism for accidents occurring in the infrastructure she oversaw during her term of office, including several deaths that occurred during a magnitude-7.1 earthquake that struck Tlalpan in 2017, Sheinbaum's political stock continued to rise. She was elected mayor of Mexico City in July 2018, receiving 50 percent of the vote in a field of seven candidates. Sheinbaum was the first woman and the first Jewish person to hold the office.

As in her earlier positions, Sheinbaum took on public transit and environmental issues. Her government expanded rainwater collection, reformed waste management, and began a reforestation program. She also announced plans to overhaul the city's subway system—long in disrepair—with massive investments in modernizing trains and shoring up existing.

infrastructure. However, her critics have pointed out the continuous deadly accidents on the subway despite her attempted reforms.

On June 12, 2023, Sheinbaum announced that she would step down as Mexico City's mayor to seek the presidency, running as a candidate for MORENA. Many see her as an ideological successor to President López Obrador (2018–24), as she has embraced similar leftist positions, such as that all citizens have basic rights to health care, education, shelter, and jobs. Sheinbaum has rejected certain aspects of the ruling party's approach to governing, however, particularly those pertaining to climate change and job creation. Whereas López Obrador stimulated economic growth by propping up Mexico's petroleum industry, Sheinbaum rejects this policy. She has pushed for a transition away from polluting fossil fuels toward nationally subsidized renewable energy.[ix]

Brandt Robinson @climberbrandt

Troublemaker Mr. Brandt Robinson, when researching him, found out that he in real life is not ok with injustice, meaning real life because I have only seen him on social media, performing history classes, this is what happens when you write down his name on a search engine:

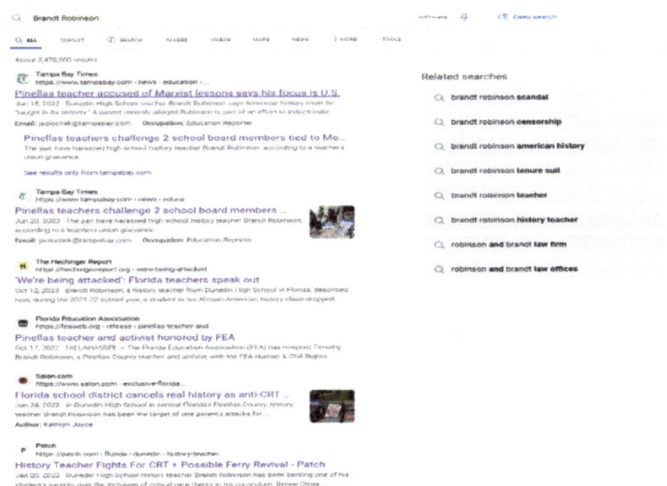

My daughter caught me laughing alone, while reading these results!

According to the Florida Education Association website, Robinson has been an educator for more than 20 years, teaching social studies and African American history. He served on the African American History Task Force for Florida, helping to create accurate and interesting curriculum for Florida's public-school students.

Robinson has a long history as an activist for human and civil rights and has dedicated his life to ending discrimination and remedying the impact of systemic racism. He has collaborated with a wide variety of organizations in pursuit of his goals, including Community Tampa Bay, Indivisible Safety Harbor, Clearwater Urban Leadership Coalition, FAST (Faith and Action for Strength Together) and Equality Florida. A member of the Pinellas Classroom Teachers Association (PCTA), Robinson has been the chair of the union's Human and Civil Rights Committee for the past eight years. Throughout his life, he has never been afraid to stand up and speak out for social justice and human and civil rights, organizing and participating in numerous protests, and speaking to official bodies such as the Pinellas County School Board many times.

In 2021, Robinson successfully pushed back when a parent accused him of "indoctrinating" students. As PCTA President Nancy Velardi describes, "Brandt believes in teaching our complete history, and spoke passionately and eloquently to our School Board, clearly explaining the role of teachers to encourage students to examine deeply all they are taught, reach their own educated conclusions, in preparation for their productive lives in a democracy." Velardi goes on to state, "I am honored to call Timothy Brandt Robinson a dear friend. I have admired him for many years, stood shoulder to shoulder with him in many of his good fights, and cannot imagine any other candidate more qualified for the FEA HCR Award this year."

Robinson was honored at the FEA Human and Civil Rights Awards Gala on Oct. 14 at the Rosen Centre Hotel in Orlando, where FEA held its annual Delegate Assembly.

The Human & Civil Rights Leadership Award was one of five statewide awards presented at the gala.[x]

This was his video I watched from him, and I realized, this gentleman is one of my heroes: **Do you know the history each made?** Available here: https://www.tiktok.com/@climberbrandt/video/7481578412575051054

TikTok Heroes | **64**

juanrodulfo.com

Dannie D. @dannie01

dannied01 Dannie D

Follow   Message

9865 Following   677.1K Followers   37.4M Likes

Leg Up News with Dannie D.
$dannied01 <my only account>

🔗 linktr.ee/DannieD01

On his social media channels, he claims to be: "Leg Up News with Dannie D. Bringing you current events with a dancing edge."

His signature move: Surprise, surpriiise!!!, and the leg up, is a distinctive move he makes to be sarcastic about everyday sad, stupid, and most of the times terrific news with source in the current administration, he alternates the surprise song with the Henry Manchini' song, the Pink Panther theme, a bursting laugh effect and other one about a beach, depending on the gravity of the new he is sharing with us.

More links: https://linktr.ee/DannieD01

Ash Dobrofsky @dashdobrofsky

According to Famous People FAQ, Dash Dobrofsky, 27, is making waves as an American political commentator, former actor, and social media influencer. Ever heard of "The Gen Z Perspective?" If not, you are about to get a crash course on its dynamic founder and host, Dash Dobrofsky. Let us get right to it!

Born and raised in sunny California, Dash grew up with his brother Spyder Dobrofsky, a movie director known for the horror film "Down Below." The Dobrofsky brothers share such a striking resemblance that they could be mistaken for twins.

Dash attended UCLA, where he earned his Bachelor of Arts degree in Political Science and minored in History, graduating in March 20231. It was not just textbooks and lectures for Dash; he dove headfirst onto the political scene, laying the groundwork for his future endeavors.

Dash's career kicked off in December 2018 when he became a literary manager at DB

Management. However, his true calling emerged in March 2020 when he founded "The Gen Z Perspective." This political media company serves up exclusive stories, unfiltered opinions, and fiery takes on culture and politics, all from the viewpoint of the younger generation.

Before his political commentary days, Dash had a notable acting career. You might have seen him in:

Children's Hospital as Justin
Modern Family as Griffin
Pyro & Klepto as Wyatt James
Superman Found Footage as Dash
Out of Focus as Graham
Bones as Chris
AwesomenessTV as Prince Adam
Mr. Student Body President as Kevin Gruber
The Stalker Club as Kyle
The Mick as "Some Guy"
Christmas Inheritance as Frankie
Spiral as Ben

On X (formerly Twitter), Dash boasts over 200,000 followers, sharing his candid political coverage and opinions. He is a prominent voice for Gen Z, advocating for issues that resonate with his peers. Dash is a vocal supporter of

President Joe Biden and often critiques former President Donald Trump. His influence is not confined to one platform—on TikTok, he has over 220,000 followers and more than seventeen million total likes. Clearly, his reach is expansive.[xi]

David Pakman
@davidpakmanshow

davidpakmanshow ✓ David Pakman

Follow   Message

738 Following   989.4K Followers   48.6M Likes

Subscribe on
Spotify | Apple Podcasts | YouTube

🔗 linktr.ee/davidpakman

David Pakman (born 2 February 1984) is an Argentine American talk show host and progressive political commentator. He is the host of the talk radio program The David Pakman Show. He was born in Buenos Aires, Argentina, and is a naturalized citizen of the United States.

David Pakman was born to a Jewish family of Ashkenazi descent in Buenos Aires in February 1984 and immigrated to the United States at the age of five. He grew up in Northampton, Massachusetts, and graduated from Northampton High School. Pakman attended the University of Massachusetts Amherst in Amherst, Massachusetts, where he majored in economics and communications. He earned an MBA degree from Bentley University in Waltham, Massachusetts.

Pakman hosts The David Pakman Show, a television, radio, and internet political program.

In 2005, Pakman began hosting a show on local radio as a "hobby", and by 2011 the show aired on one hundred stations, and outlets including DirecTV and DISH Network through Free Speech TV, the PACIFICA Radio Network, on YouTube, LBRY, and via podcasts. The program first aired in August 2005 on WXOJ-LP ("Valley Free Radio"), located in Northampton, Massachusetts, as Midweek Politics with David Pakman.

Pakman has appeared on Fox News, CNN, HLN's Nancy Grace program, HLN's Dr. Drew on Call, the Lex Fridman Podcast, two episodes of The Joe Rogan Experience, Piers Morgan Uncensored, Mother Jones, the Boston Herald, The New York Times, and Wired.

Pakman earns income through sales to advertisers, ads on platforms including YouTube and memberships sold through his website.

In June 2024, Pakman announced he was ending his radio and television show in August and would instead focus his efforts on digital content, such as his YouTube show.

Pakman announced that he would be taking paternity leave in June 2022 after the birth of his first child, a daughter.

Bibliography

Think Like a Detective: A Kid's Guide to Critical Thinking (2023)

Think Like a Scientist: A Kid's Guide to Scientific Thinking (2023)

Think Like a Voter: A Kid's Guide to Shaping Our Country's Future (2024)

The Echo Machine: How Right-Wing Extremism Created a Post-Truth America (2025)[xii]

CDejavu @dejavu_candy

So, few I could find, these are more links: https://linktr.ee/Dejavu_Candy

Eden @edensingsofficial

On her YouTube channel found this about her: *"I am a professional singer and songwriter! I reword songs that carry cultural significance and adapt them to current events."*

More links: https://linktr.ee/edensings

Facts to Grind @factstogrind

This is it:

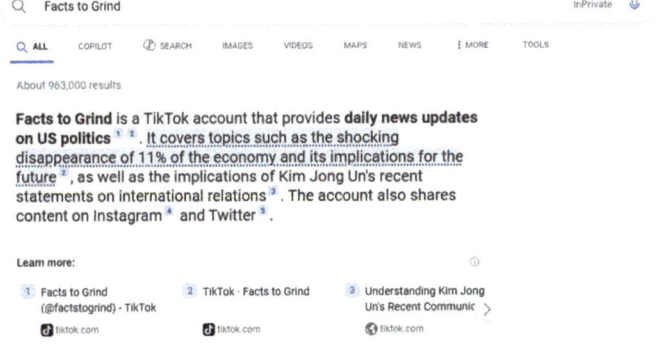

Hal_for_NY__ @hal_for_ny__

On his YouTube account, I found this: *"I do short form political videos covering the topics of the day. Left Leaning independent, and former Congressional Candidate."*

Nothing more...

Bootsy Sanders @he.cold3

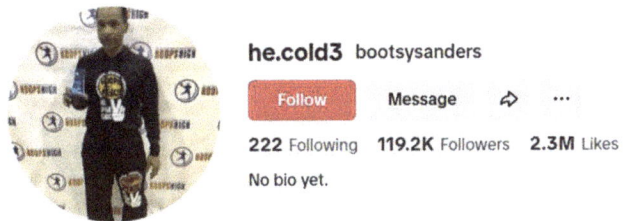

He wants to keep it anonymous.

LEIGH MCGOWAN @IAMPOLITICSGIRL

Leigh McGowan launched PoliticsGirl as a way to help people reconnect with politics. She started the YouTube channel in 2015 as a way to inform and inspire because she said, "when you understand you care, and when you care you vote". After watching the fallout from the Trump years, Leigh relaunched the project on TikTok in September of 2020 doing rants in her kitchen to engage the younger generation whose participation, she believed, was essential to the future of the country. People loved her no-nonsense, casual approach and the way she was able to break down complicated issues into everyday speech. As her numbers grew so did her popularity and influence. People like her because she is smart in a way that does not make them feel dumb. She is able to put into words what people are thinking, or she is thinking what people cannot quite put into words. Leigh is now on TikTok, Twitter (X), Threads, and Instagram as @IAmPoliticsGirl and PoliticsGirl on YouTube & Facebook. With almost two million followers, her rants now have hundreds of millions of views, and she is supported by everyone from leading politicians and celebrities to a deep cross-section of the American public. She has been featured in multiple publications and her rants have been played entirety numerous times on national news broadcasts like MSNBC's the 11th Hour. The rants were also the inspiration for the extremely popular PoliticsGirl Podcast, which launched as a weekly download in audio and visual form in November of 2021, and has featured everyone from White House Chief of Staff, Ron Klain, to Broadway & Television Superstar, Alexandra Billings. Her standalone episodes, without guests, explain complicated issues in a way the public can understand, and has touched on subjects ranging from the "History of Public Education in America" to "The Rise of Autocracy Around the World." Leigh writes, researches and performs all her own pieces, and has truly inspired the country, and the world at large, to reengage with American politics. Her work is now credited with making a difference to everything from election results to public opinion and she has now been to the White House on multiple occasions to meet with the President and his staff because of that influence. Her work during the 2022 midterms with from everyone to Democrats Abroad and The States Project, to individual campaigns, can be seen to have made a discernible difference to results.

Ultimately Leigh honestly believes in the American experiment, and trusts that we can fix what is broken. The county might be sitting at a terrifying crossroad, but she sees it as an opportunity and subscribes to the idea that no matter what we have been taught, EVERYONE should be talking about politics. Not caring about government does not mean their decisions do not affect you, it means you can't affect them. And it is about time 'We the People' had some say over our own lives, and that all starts with understanding.[xiii]

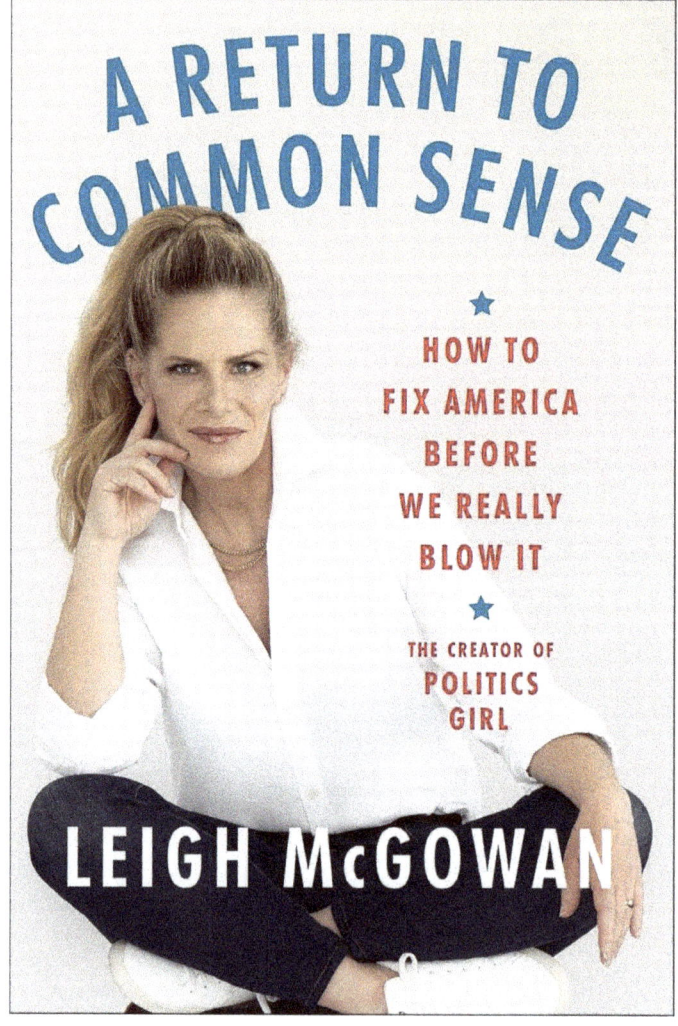

Her book is available here:

juanrodulfo.com

Isa Bako @isa_bako

isa_bako Isa Bako

Follow Message

7 Following **44.6K** Followers **629.1K** Likes

This is my main now. Other account was banned

🔗 www.patreon.com/ahfreaq?u...

No too much data about Bako...

JARED VAN @JAREDVANEDUCATION

jaredvaneducation @jaredvaneducation

Follow Message

1041 Following   19.8K Followers   231.4K Likes

PhD student in Special Education. Abolitionist. Stumbling through life. 🖤✊🏾

bio.site/jaredvan

According to his bio.site: Behavior Scientist, BCBA, Precision Teacher, and a PhD Student at Penn State, Black, and here to educate.

On his website I found this: *I am currently a PhD Student at The Pennsylvania State University under the supervision of Dr. Richard M. Kubina Jr. in the Special Education Department. I received my M.S. in Applied Behavior Analysis at The Chicago School of Professional Psychology and I am currently a Board-Certified Behavior Analyst (BCBA).*

I have worked as a behavior interventionist in the California Bay Area and greater Los Angeles Area for over half a decade working with a diverse population of clients with autism and other developmental disabilities.

My current research interests are in the areas of Precision Teaching, Behavior Analysis, Instructional Design, and Education Policy.[xiv]

JASMINE CROCKETT @JASMINEFORUS

Congresswoman Jasmine Crockett has purposefully made every decision with one goal in mind: protecting the civil liberties of those in underrepresented communities. As a public defender, civil rights attorney, State Representative, and United States Congresswoman, Jasmine Crockett dedicates her life to public service, with the goal of serving justice and ensuring equality for all.

During political turmoil, economic distress, and racial inequality, Congresswoman Crockett laced up her shoes to march for justice and run for the Texas House of Representatives. The sole Black freshman and youngest Black lawmaker in Texas during the 87th Legislative Session, Congresswoman Crockett navigated what has been marked as the most conservative session in Texas history. Despite the uphill climb, Congresswoman Crockett filed more bills than any other freshman, assembled a wide coalition to pass landmark criminal justice reforms in the House, and brought more accessibility and accountability to her office than before. She was a founding member of both the Texas

Progressive Caucus as well as the Texas Caucus on Climate, Energy, and the Environment. As State Representative, she fought for economic opportunity as a member of the Business & Industry Committee and advocated for reform on the Criminal Jurisprudence Committee. Congresswoman Crockett was one of the lead architects of the 2021 Texas House Quorum Break, which brought attention to the draconian and restrictive voting measures being proposed in the legislature.

Her passion for justice and the protection of people's rights led her to pursue a career as a public defender, and civil rights and criminal defense attorney. She focused on defending our most vulnerable among us from exploitation in the criminal justice system. As she began her career in the Bowie County Public Defender's Office, Congresswoman Crockett worked tirelessly to keep children safe and out of jail. Her time there serves as a reminder that criminal justice is an intersectional issue.

Following her service in the Texas Legislature, Congresswoman Jasmine Crockett has served as the U.S. Representative for Texas 30th Congressional District since January 2023, representing portions of Dallas and Tarrant counties, representing the seat previously held for 30 years by the late Congresswoman Eddie Bernice Johnson. In the 118th Congress, Congresswoman Crockett was elected as

Freshman Leadership Representative, and in the 119th Congress she was appointed to the position of Vice Ranking Member of the House Committee on Oversight and Government Reform and the Ranking Member of the House Judiciary Subcommittee on Oversight. She currently serves on the House Judiciary Committee and the House Committee on Oversight and Government Reform. She was also appointed as Communications Task Force Co-Chair for the Democratic Women's Caucus.

Congresswoman Crockett earned her B.A. in Business Administration from Rhodes College and her J.D. from the University of Houston. She is licensed to practice law in Texas, Arkansas, and Federal Courts. Crockett is the past Bowie County Democratic Party Chair, held various leadership positions within the legal community, is a former board member of the Dallas County Metrocare Services, and is a proud member of Delta Sigma Theta Sorority, Incorporated.[xv]

JOY ANN REID @JOYREIDOFFICIAL

Joy-Ann M. Lomena-Reid (née Lomena; born December 8, 1968) is an American political commentator and television host. She was a national correspondent for MSNBC and is best known for hosting the political commentary program The ReidOut from 2020 to 2025. Her previous anchoring credits include The Reid Report (2014–2015) and AM Joy (2016–2020). The New York Times described Reid as a "heroine" emerging from the political movements and protests against Donald Trump. She has written three books: Fracture: Barack Obama, the Clintons, and the Racial Divide (2016), The Man Who Sold America: Trump and the Unraveling of the American Story (2019), and Medgar and Myrlie: Medgar Evers and the Love Story That Awakened America (2024).

Reid was born Joy-Ann Lomena in Brooklyn, New York City. Her father was from the Democratic Republic of Congo, and her mother a college professor and nutritionist from

Guyana. Her parents met in graduate school at the University of Iowa in Iowa City. Reid was raised Methodist and has one sister and one brother. Her father was an engineer who was mostly absent from the family; her parents eventually divorced, and her father returned to Congo. She was raised mostly in Denver, Colorado, until the age of seventeen, when her mother died of breast cancer and she moved to Flatbush, Brooklyn, to live with an aunt. Reid graduated from Harvard University in 1991 with a concentration in film studies.

In a 2013 interview, Reid recalled that her college experience was a quick immersion into a demographically opposite place from where she lived, from a community that was eighty percent African American to a community that was six percent African American. She had to learn to live with roommates and people who were not her family. She paid her own bills and tuition while at Harvard and said it was a good learning and growing experience overall.

Reid began her journalism career in 1997, leaving New York and her job at a business consulting firm to begin working in South Florida for a WSVN Channel 7 morning show. She left journalism in 2003 to work with the group America Coming Together to oppose the Iraq War and President George W. Bush. She later returned to broadcasting as a talk radio host and worked on Barack Obama's 2008 presidential campaign.

From 2006 to 2007, Reid was the co-host of Wake Up South Florida, a morning radio talk show broadcast from Radio One's then-Miami affiliate WTPS, alongside "James T" Thomas. She served as managing editor of The Grio (2011–2014), a political columnist for Miami Herald (2003–2015), and the editor of The Reid Report political blog (2000–2014).

From February 2014 to February 2015, Reid hosted her own MSNBC afternoon cable news show, The Reid Report. The show was canceled on February 19, 2015, and Reid was shifted to a new role as an MSNBC national correspondent. Beginning in May 2016, Reid hosted AM Joy, a political weekend-morning talk show on MSNBC, and was a frequent substitute for other MSNBC hosts, including Chris Hayes and Rachel Maddow. As of 2018, Reid's morning show on Saturdays averaged nearly one million weekly viewers.

In 2017, Reid ranked fourth among Twitter's top tweeted news outlets and most tweeted journalist at each outlet. The Daily Dot credited her in August of that year with coining the term KHive for supporters of Kamala Harris.

In July 2020, MSNBC announced that Reid would host The ReidOut, a new Washington-based weeknight commentary show in the 7 p.m. Eastern time slot vacated by the March

2020 retirement of Hardball host Chris Matthews, making her cable's first Black female primetime anchor. On February 23, 2025, The New York Times reported that MSNBC had canceled The ReidOut, with plans to air its final episode during the week of February 24-28. The final broadcast of The ReidOut would air on February 24, 2025.

Reid also teaches a Syracuse University class in Manhattan exploring race, gender, and the media.[xvi]

Lisa Yahne @lisayay1966

On linktr.ee is described as: Artist, crafter, teacher, progressive.
More links: https://linktr.ee/lisayay

Michael David Gantt
@mdg65Ohawk7thacct

I find such an affinity between Michael and my uncle "Theo," beyond their physical match, their hair, their face, is their critical point of view about life and its actors.

I watch Michael and is like watching Theo speaking English...

The speed of their speech, the deep on their voices, men...!

The real name of @mdg650hawk is Michael David Gantt, born on August 28, 1995, in Wichita Falls, Texas. Michael grew up with a passion for performing arts, which led him to pursue a career in entertainment. Before becoming a TikTok sensation, Michael worked as a professional dancer and actor, performing in various shows and musicals.

Michael joined TikTok in 2019, initially posting dance and lip-sync videos. His early content gained traction, and he quickly built a following. mdg650hawk's unique style, which combines his dancing skills with comedic timing, resonated with audiences, and his popularity grew exponentially.

So, what makes mdg650hawk's content so unique? Here are some key elements that contribute to his success:

• Dancing: Michael's background in dance is evident in his TikTok videos, which highlight his impressive choreography skills.

• Comedy: @mdg650hawk's humor is a major factor in his popularity. He often incorporates comedy into his videos, making them entertaining and engaging.

• Storytelling: Michael's videos often tell a story, which keeps his audience engaged and curious to see what happens next.

- Authenticity: @mdg650hawk's content is genuine and authentic, which has helped him build a strong connection with his followers.

Despite his growing fame, Michael remains private about his personal life. He has kept his relationships and family life out of the spotlight, focusing on his career and content creation. However, he has shared glimpses of his life, including his love for video games and music, which has helped his followers connect with him on a more personal level.

@mdg650hawk's popularity has led to collaborations with other TikTok creators and brands. He has worked with brands such as Funko, G Fuel, and HyperX, promoting their products and services to his massive following. His collaborations have not only expanded his reach but also provided him with opportunities to create content that resonates with his audience.

@mdg650hawk's influence extends beyond TikTok. He has inspired a generation of young creators to pursue their passions and build their online presence. His content has also had a positive impact on his followers, providing entertainment, inspiration, and a sense of community.

In conclusion, @mdg650hawk, whose real name is Michael David Gantt, is a talented TikTok creator who has built a massive following with his unique content. His passion for dance, comedy, and storytelling has resonated with audiences worldwide, making him a household name. As he continues to create and innovate, it is exciting to see what the future holds for this talented creator.[xvii]

MercurialLuvr @mercurialluvr

mercurialluvr MercurialLuvr HT

Follow | Message

133 Following   **120.9K** Followers   **4.6M** Likes

I Roll Better Than U 😋 😮‍💨
God 1st
BIG ♊
NYC 🗽
Bluesky/RedNote: MercurialLuvr

No so much information about available

Mercedes Chandler
@mercychandler

mercychandler Mercedes Chandler

Follow   Message

534 Following   **535.7K** Followers   **7.7M** Likes

● ATX 🌹 HUMANIST
WANT TO COLLAB? 🌱 👊 👊 🌱
OfficialCampCallout@gmail.com

🔗 linktr.ee/campcallout

On Instagram I found: "Humanist, ex-conservative turned liberal."
More links: https://linktr.ee/campcallout

REID MOON @MOONSRAREBOOKS

Books and their role saving democracy and by proxy, our planet? Only light can defeat darkness...

Reid Moon is the owner and collector of the treasures at Moon's Rare Books, a bucket-list bookstore in Provo, Utah. Reid began his bookselling career after a brief stint in the insurance business. After that, Reid took over his family's small community bookstore in Dallas. It had been in operation since 1975 but had remained a small "mom and pop" bookshop. Over the next twenty-five years, Reid gradually grew the business, selling both old and new books at bookstores in Dallas and Los Angeles before moving to Provo, Utah in 2015; at which time he transitioned from "new and used" to "used and rare" books only.

He is a "storyteller" that enjoys sharing the history behind the thousands of books, documents, and artifacts he has collected over the past three decades. Mr. Moon began sharing his stories daily on social media in 2022, which has expanded his reach to a world-wide audience and made Moon's Rare Books a "bucket-list" bookstore.

If you would like to meet Reid, join us for one of our Show and Tell Events at our Bookstore in Provo, UT! Refer to our "Events" page for more information on these one-of-a-kind events!

Moon's Rare Books is located at 4801 N University Ave #340, Provo, UT 84604.[xviii]

Neil deGrasse Tyson
@neildegrassetyson

Science and knowledge and their role saving democracy and by proxy our planet? Only light can defeat darkness...

Neil deGrasse Tyson, born October 5, 1958, is an American astrophysicist, author, and science communicator. Tyson studied at Harvard University, the University of Texas at Austin, and Columbia University. From 1991 to 1994, he was a postdoctoral research associate at Princeton University. In 1994, he joined the Hayden Planetarium as a staff scientist and the Princeton faculty as a visiting research scientist and lecturer. In 1996, he became director of the planetarium and oversaw its $210 million reconstruction project, which was completed in 2000. Since 1996, he has been the director of the Hayden Planetarium at the Rose Center for Earth and Space in New York City. The center is part of the American Museum of Natural History, where Tyson founded the Department of Astrophysics in 1997 and has been a research associate in the department since 2003.

From 1995 to 2005, Tyson authored monthly essays in the "Universe" column for Natural History magazine, some of which were later published in his books Death by Black Hole (2007) and Astrophysics for People in a Hurry (2017). During the same period, he wrote a monthly column in StarDate magazine, answering questions about the universe under the pen name "Merlin". Material from the column appeared in his books Merlin's Tour of the Universe (1998) and Just Visiting This Planet (1998). Tyson served on a 2001 government commission on the future of the U.S. aerospace industry and on the 2004 Moon, Mars and Beyond commission. He was awarded the NASA Distinguished Public Service Medal in the same year. From 2006 to 2011, he hosted the television show NOVA ScienceNow on PBS. Since 2009, Tyson has hosted the weekly podcast StarTalk. A spin-off, also called StarTalk, began airing on National Geographic in 2015. In 2014, he hosted the television series Cosmos: A Spacetime Odyssey, a successor to Carl Sagan's 1980 series Cosmos: A Personal Voyage. The U.S. National Academy of Sciences awarded Tyson the Public Welfare Medal in 2015 for his "extraordinary role in exciting the public about the wonders of science".

Tyson was born in Manhattan as the second of three children, into a Catholic family living in the Bronx. His father, Cyril deGrasse Tyson (1927–2016), was a sociologist and human resource commissioner for New York City mayor John Lindsay, and the first director of Harlem Youth Opportunities Unlimited. His mother, Sunchita Maria Tyson (née Feliciano; 1928–2023), was a gerontologist for the U.S. Department of Health, Education and Welfare and is of Puerto Rican descent. Neil has two siblings: Stephen Joseph Tyson and Lynn Antipas Tyson. Neil's middle name, deGrasse, is from the maiden name of his paternal grandmother, who was born as Altima de Grasse in the British West Indies Island of Nevis.

Tyson graduated from The Bronx High School of Science in 1976 where he was captain of the wrestling team and editor-in-chief of the Physical Science Journal. His interest in astronomy began at the age of nine after visiting the sky theater of the Hayden Planetarium. He recalled that "so strong was that imprint (of the night sky) that I'm certain that I had no choice in the matter, that in fact, the universe called me." During high school, Tyson attended astronomy courses offered by the Hayden Planetarium, which he called "the most formative period" of his life. He credited Mark Chartrand III, director of the planetarium at the time, as his "first intellectual role model" and his enthusiastic teaching style mixed with humor inspired Tyson to communicate the universe to others the way he did.

When he was fourteen, he received a scholarship from the Explorers Club of New York to view the June 1973 total solar eclipse aboard the SS Canberra. The scientific cruise carried out two thousand scientists, engineers, and enthusiasts, including Neil Armstrong, Scott Carpenter, and Isaac Asimov.

Tyson obsessively studied astronomy in his teen years; he eventually even gained some fame in the astronomy community by giving lectures on the subject at the age of fifteen. Astronomer Carl Sagan, who was a faculty member at Cornell University, tried to recruit Tyson to Cornell for undergraduate studies. In his book, The Sky Is Not the Limit, Tyson wrote:

My letter of application had been dripping with an interest in the universe. The admission office, unbeknownst to me, had forwarded my application for Carl Sagan's attention. Within weeks, I received a personal letter...

Tyson revisited this moment on his first episode of Cosmos: A Spacetime Odyssey. Pulling out a 1975 calendar belonging to the famous astronomer, he found the day Sagan invited the 17-year-old to spend a day in Ithaca. Sagan had offered to put him up for the night if his bus back to the Bronx did not come. Tyson said, "I already knew I wanted to become a scientist. But that afternoon, I learned from Carl the kind of person I wanted to become."

Tyson has written and broadcast extensively about his views of science, spirituality, and the spirituality of science, including the essays "The Perimeter of Ignorance" and "Holy Wars", both appearing in Natural History magazine and the 2006 Beyond Belief workshop. In an interview with comedian Paul Mecurio, Tyson offered his definition of spirituality, "For me, when I say spiritual, I'm referring to a feeling you would have that connects you to the universe in a way that it may defy simple vocabulary. We think about the universe as an intellectual playground, which it surely is, but the moment you learn something that touches an emotion rather than just something intellectual, I would call that a spiritual encounter with the universe." He has argued that many great historical scientists' belief in intelligent design limited their scientific inquiries to the detriment of the advance of scientific knowledge.

When asked during a question session at the University at Buffalo if he believed in a higher power, Tyson responded: "Every account of a higher power that I've seen described, of all religions that I've seen, include many statements with regard to the benevolence of that power. When I look at the universe and all the ways the universe wants to kill us, I find it hard to reconcile that with statements of beneficence."

In an interview with Big Think, he said: "So, what people are really after is what is my stance on religion or spirituality or God, and I would say if I find a word that came closest, it would be 'agnostic'... at the end of the day I'd rather not be any category at all." Additionally, in the same interview with Big Think, Tyson mentioned that he edited Wikipedia's entry on him to include the fact that he is an agnostic:

Atheists constantly claim me. I find this intriguing. In fact, on my Wiki page —I did not create the Wiki page. Others did, and I am flattered that people cared enough about my life to assemble it—and it said, "Neil deGrasse Tyson is an atheist." I said, "Well, that's not really true." I said, "Neil deGrasse Tyson is an agnostic." I went back a week later. It said, "Neil deGrasse Tyson is an atheist" again—within a week! —and I said, "What's up with that?" and I said, "All right, I have to word it a little differently." So, I said, "Okay, Neil deGrasse Tyson, widely claimed by atheists, is actually an agnostic."

During the interview "Called by the Universe: A Conversation with Neil deGrasse Tyson" in 2009, Tyson said: "I can't agree to the claims by atheists that I'm one of that community. I do not have the time, energy, or interest of conducting myself that way... I am not trying to convert people. I do not care.

Tyson in conversation with Richard Dawkins at Howard University, 2010

In March 2014, philosopher and secularism proponent Massimo Pigliucci asked Tyson: "What is it you think about God?" Tyson replied: "I remain unconvinced by any claims anyone has ever made about the existence or the power of a divine force operating in the universe." Pigliucci then asked him why he expressed discomfort with the label "atheist" in his Big Think video. Tyson replied by reiterating his dislike for one-word labels, saying: "That's what adjectives are for. What kind of atheist are you? Are you an ardent atheist? Are you a passive atheist? An apathetic atheist? Do you really, or do you just not even care? So, I would be on the 'I really don't care' side of that, if you had to find adjectives to put in front of the word 'atheist'."

Pigliucci contrasted Tyson with scientist Richard Dawkins: "(Dawkins) really does consider, at this point, himself to be an atheist activist. You very clearly made the point that you are not." Tyson replied: "I completely respect that activity. He's fulfilling a really important role out there." Tyson has spoken about philosophy on numerous occasions. In March 2014, during an episode of The Nerdist Podcast, he said that philosophy is "useless" and that a philosophy major "can really mess you up", which was met with disapproval. Pigliucci, a philosopher, later criticized him for "dismissing philosophy as a useless enterprise".

In 2005, at a conference at the National Academy of Sciences, Tyson responded to a question about whether genetic differences might keep women from working as scientists. He said that his goal to become an astrophysicist was "hands down the path of most resistance through the forces... of society... My life experience tells me, when you do not find Blacks in the sciences, when you do not find women in the sciences, I know these forces are real and I had to survive them to get where I am today. So, before we start talking about genetic differences, you have to produce a system where there's equal opportunity. Then we can start having that conversation."

In a 2014 interview with Grantland, Tyson said that he related his experience on that 2005 panel to make the point that the scientific question about genetic differences cannot be answered until the social barriers are dismantled. "I'm saying before you even have that conversation, you have to be really sure that access to opportunity has been level." In the same interview, Tyson said that race is not a part of the point he is trying to make in his career or with his life. According to Tyson, "That then becomes the point of people's understanding of me, rather than the astrophysics. So, it is a failed educational step for that to be the case. If you end up being distracted by that and not (getting) the message." He purposefully no longer speaks publicly about race. "I don't give talks on it. I do not even give Black History Month talks. I decline every single one of them. In fact, since 1993, I've declined every interview that has my being black as the premise of the interview."

Tyson has positively advocated for the freedoms of homosexual and transgender people and argued about the topic repeatedly against right-wing commentators.[xix]

Jon_48 @openlyblack

openlyblack Jon_48

Follow | Message

9993 Following **43.8K** Followers **2.7M** Likes

Born in the 40's; raised in the 50's; learned & marched in the 60's;

Born in the 40's; raised in the 50's; learned and marched in the 60's.

I would add: And now, here we are again with the same predicaments, my respected @openlyblack friend.

Alex Pearlman @pearlmania500

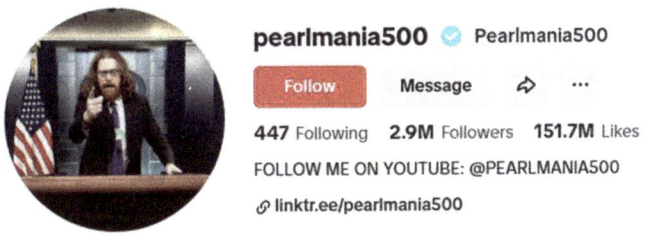

At the BING search results says: *"The ranting comedian who yells the news at you."* Here are more links: https://linktr.ee/pearlmania500

PissedMagistus @pissedmagistus

More links: https://linktr.ee/pissedmagistus

PissedoffBartender
@PISSEDOFFBARTENDER

pissedoffbartender Pissedoffbartender

Follow | Message

569 Following   691.8K Followers   11.7M Likes

YT AND TWITCH BELOW, LIVE MON-FRI @6

code PISSEDOFF 15% off @ Getgoodlife.com

🔗 linktr.ee/pissedoffbartender

The description on YouTube says:

"I am just a dude trying to find himself on the right side of history. I am a husband, father, and heavy armored fighter in the SCA."

His signature movement is the walk, and two times fast-forward talk along his backyard fence, and his slogan:

"Keep the motherfucking boots out of your motherfucking mouth and remember that the golden rule will always remain YEEHAW FUCK THE LAW, I love you'all I'll, see ya down the line."

More links:
https://linktr.ee/pissedoffbartender

Mike M @RATIONALBOOMER

rationalboomer rationalboomer

Follow   Message

10K Following   **450K** Followers   **22.3M** Likes

Mike
P.O Box 148
Mound. MN. 55364
Rational Boomer Podcast link below

🔗 youtube.com/@rationalboomer

More links:
https://www.youtube.com/@rationalboomer

ROBERT REICH @RBREICH

rbreich ✓ Robert Reich

Follow   Message

142 Following   1.1M Followers   19.5M Likes

UC Berkeley professor, former Secretary of Labor, co-founder, @inequalitymedia

🔗 linktr.ee/rbreich

Robert Bernard Reich, born June 24, 1946, is an American professor, author, lawyer, and political commentator. He worked in the administrations of presidents Gerald Ford and Jimmy Carter and served as Secretary of Labor from 1993 to 1997 in the cabinet of President Bill Clinton. He was also a member of President Barack Obama's economic transition advisory board.

Reich has been the Chancellor's Professor of Public Policy at the Goldman School of Public Policy at UC Berkeley since January 2006. He was formerly a lecturer at Harvard University's John F. Kennedy School of Government and a professor of social and economic policy at the Heller School for Social Policy and Management of Brandeis University. In 2008, Time magazine named him one of the Ten Best Cabinet Members of the century, and in the same year The Wall Street Journal placed him sixth on its list of Most Influential Business Thinkers.

Reich has published numerous books, including the best-sellers The Work of Nations (1991),

Reason (2004), Supercapitalism (2007), Aftershock (2010), Beyond Outrage (2012), and Saving Capitalism (2015). The Robert Reich–Jacob Kornbluth film Saving Capitalism debuted on Netflix in November 2017, and their film Inequality for All won a U.S. Documentary Special Jury Award for Achievement in Filmmaking at the 2013 Sundance Film Festival. He is board chair emeritus of Common Cause and blogs at Robertreich.org.

In an interview with The New York Times in 2008, Reich explained that "I don't believe in redistribution of wealth for the sake of redistributing wealth. But I am concerned about how we can afford to pay for what we as a nation need to do (...) (Taxes should pay) for what we need to be safe and productive. As Oliver Wendell Holmes once wrote, 'taxes are the price we pay for a civilized society.'"

In response to a question as to what to recommend to the incoming president regarding a fair and sustainable income and wealth distribution, Reich said: "Expand the Earned Income Tax Credit—a wage supplement for lower-income people, and finance it with a higher marginal income tax on the top five percent. For the longer term, invest in education for lower income communities, starting with early-childhood education and extending all the way up to better access to post-secondary education."

Reich is pro-union, saying: "Unionization is not just good for workers in unions, unionization is very, very important for the economy overall, and would create broad benefits for the United States." Writing in 2014, he stated that he favors raising the federal minimum wage to $15/hr across three years, believing that it will not adversely impact big business, and will increase higher value worker availability.

Reich also supports unconditional and universal basic income. On the eve of a June 2016 popular vote in Switzerland on basic income, he declared that countries would have to introduce this instrument eventually.

While affordable housing has been a central issue in Reich's activism, in July 2020 Reich opposed a high-density development project in his own neighborhood in Berkeley. He supported making a 120-year-old triplex a landmark to prevent the construction of a 10-apartment building, one of which would be deed restricted to being rented to a low-income tenant, citing "the character of the neighborhood". During an interview with W. Kamau Bell the following month, Reich reaffirmed his support for affordable housing "in every community I've been involved in" and critiqued the development for replacing the house with "condos selling for one and a half million dollars each".

Although a supporter of Israel, Reich has criticized Israel's settlement building in the occupied Palestinian territories. More recently, Reich has spoken out against the "bloodbath" in Gaza, and declared "we must restrict U.S. arms sales to Israel."[xx]

Ro Khanna @REPROKHANNA

reprokhanna ✓ Rep. Ro Khanna

Follow Message

502 Following **521.2K** Followers **10.7M** Likes

Representative from Silicon Valley's CA-17 in Congress

Congressman Ro Khanna represents California's 17th Congressional District, located in the heart of Silicon Valley, and is serving his fourth term.

Rep. Khanna serves on the House Armed Services Committee as ranking member of the Subcommittee on Cyber, Innovative Technologies and Information Systems (CITI), as co-chair of the Congressional Caucus on India and Indian Americans, a member of the Select Committee on the Strategic Competition between the United States and the Chinese Communist Party, and on the Oversight and Accountability Committee, where he previously chaired the Environmental Subcommittee.

As a leading progressive in the House, Rep, Khanna is working to restore American manufacturing and technology leadership, improve the lives of working people, and advance U.S. leadership on climate, human rights, and diplomacy around the world.[xxi]

ROBERT GARCIA @ROBERTGARCIA

Congressman Robert Garcia is a career educator and former Mayor of Long Beach, currently serving his second term representing Long Beach to Southeast Los Angeles in Congress. Congressman Garcia was elected Caucus Leadership Representative by his Democratic colleagues, is Ranking Member of the National Security, Border and Foreign Affairs Subcommittee on the Oversight Committee, and is a proud member of the Congressional Progressive, Hispanic and Equality Caucuses.

In his first term, Congressman Garcia championed the pro-housing movement in Congress to encourage the development of new housing units and bring down the cost of living across the nation. Congressman Garcia was instrumental in founding and launching the bipartisan Congressional Yes In My Back Yard (YIMBY) Caucus, aimed at promoting policies to increase the housing supply to address affordability and homelessness.

In the 118th Congress, two bills introduced by Congressman Garcia were signed by President Joe Biden into law. These bipartisan laws, aimed at improving government efficiency, will save taxpayer dollars and promote more accountable government operations.

As Caucus Leadership Representative, Congressman Garcia is a key figure in steering the direction and priorities of the Democratic Caucus in the U.S. House. Congressman Garcia communicates between party leadership and newer members to ensure that the voices of Representatives across the party are heard and represented in legislation.

Congressman Garcia is also the co-chair of the Congressional Ports Opportunity, Renewal, Trade, and Security (PORTS) Caucus and Peru Caucus. The PORTS Caucus advocates for port infrastructure, secure and resilient supply chains, and for our nation's economy. The Peru Caucus aims to strengthen the relationship between the United States and Peruvian people by enhancing political dialogue and cooperation on shared values and principles.

Congressman Garcia was elected to represent California's 42nd Congressional District, including Long Beach and Southeast Los Angeles, in November 2022. Congressman Garcia previously served as the 28th Mayor of Long Beach from 2014 to 2022 and served on the City Council from 2009 to 2014.

Congressman Garcia believes in defending our democracy, leveling the playing field with progressive education policy, addressing the climate crisis, supporting working families with increasing wages, and fighting to expand and protect essential rights for women, immigrants, and the LGBTQ+ community. In Congress, Congressman Garcia has championed legislation to tackle the affordable housing shortage, make our government run more efficiently, regulate ammunition sales to address our gun violence epidemic, reduce ocean shipping pollution, pandemic preparedness, and defend international human rights.

Congressman Garcia is proud to serve as the first openly LGBTQ immigrant in Congress. A self-admitted comic book nerd, Congressman Garcia credits comics with helping him learn to read and write English and has since channeled his love of popular culture into founding the Congressional Popular Arts Caucus, which celebrates the economic and cultural contributions of the popular arts.

Congressman Garcia immigrated from Peru to the United States as a young child and was raised in Southern California, and became a U.S. citizen in his 20's. He holds an M.A. from the University of Southern California and an Ed.D. in Higher Education from Cal State Long Beach, where he also earned his B.A. in Communications.[xxii]

Sir Addison Witt
@SIRADDISONWITT

siraddisonwitt Addi's Friends

[Follow] [Message]

1994 Following   **33.3K** Followers   **278.4K** Likes

actor, poet, teacher.
https://www.siraddisonwitt.com

🔗 www.siraddisonwitt.com

Addison Witt is a distinguished actor, speaker, and mentor with an extensive career spanning TV, film, stage, and commercials. Formerly a Hollywood talent manager and agent, Addison has worked with some of the biggest names in the entertainment industry, shaping careers and guiding artists toward success. His keen eye for talent and deep understanding of the business have made him a sought-after industry expert.

In addition to his work in entertainment, Addison is the Co-Chair of the Defense of Democracy Film Festival, where he champions films that inspire change and uphold democratic values. His commitment to storytelling extends beyond acting—he believes in using media as a powerful tool for education, empowerment, and advocacy.

As a respected acting coach, Addison has helped countless performers refine their craft, particularly in the competitive world of commercial acting. His teaching style is dynamic, engaging, and deeply rooted in his real-world experience. Whether coaching seasoned professionals or emerging talent, Addison provides invaluable insights that help actors navigate and excel in the industry.

Now, in addition to acting and teaching, Addison is embarking on an inspirational speaking tour, sharing his journey of faith, perseverance, and purpose with audiences across the country. His mission is to empower others to step into their potential with clarity and conviction.

From managing Hollywood stars to teaching aspiring performers, from acting on screen to advocating for impactful storytelling—Addison Witt's journey is one of dedication, resilience, and a lifelong commitment to the arts and personal growth.[xxiii]

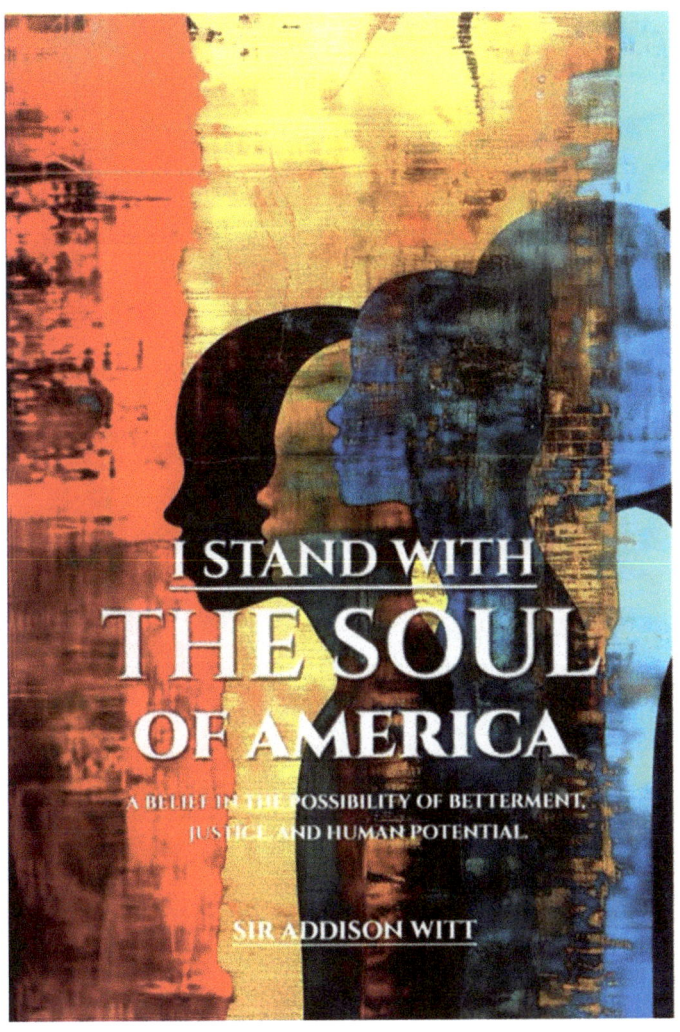

His most recent book is available here:

STACEY ABRAMS @STACEYABRAMS

Stacey Abrams (born December 9, 1973, Madison, Wisconsin, U.S.) is an American politician, lawyer, activist, and writer who is an influential figure in the Democratic Party, especially known for her work involving voter rights. She gained national prominence in 2018 when she ran unsuccessfully for governor of Georgia, becoming the first Black woman to win a major party's gubernatorial nomination. Abrams was also the Democratic nominee in the 2022 race, but she was again defeated.

Abrams began her career as a tax lawyer in Atlanta. In 2002, when she was 29 years old, she became Atlanta's deputy city attorney, and in that role she led more than twenty attorneys and paralegals. In 2006 Abrams was elected to the Georgia House of Representatives, representing a district in Atlanta. In 2010 she made history when she became the first African American to serve as minority leader in the House. During her tenure, Abrams established the New Georgia Project (2014), which sought to register voters, particularly young people, and people of color. In addition, she played a key role in defeating a tax reform bill (2011) that she noted would raise taxes on the middle class. In 2017 Abrams resigned from the House to enter the governor's race.

On the campaign trail, Abrams called for greater access to health care and new investment in public schools. She also supported abortion rights and gun control. Backed by Bernie Sanders and other prominent Democrats, Abrams won the party's primary. She faced off against the Republican nominee, Brian Kemp, who was the secretary of state, in charge of elections. The hotly contested race drew national attention. Abrams was endorsed by Barack Obama and made a campaign appearance with Oprah Winfrey. Despite such high-profile support, Abrams narrowly lost to Kemp in the 2018 election, 50.2 percent to 48.8 percent. However, she controversially refused to concede, noting allegations of voter suppression.

Shortly after the loss, Abrams founded (2018) Fair Fight Action to protect voter rights. She also was engaged in efforts to increase voter turnout. In 2019 Abrams became the first Black woman to give the State of the Union response as she delivered her party's rebuttal to U.S. Pres.

Donald Trump's speech. Later that year she opted not to run for the U.S. Senate or the presidency and instead focused on securing the election of other Democratic candidates. As part of her work, she established Fair Fight 2020. After Joe Biden won the Democratic nomination for president, Abrams was reportedly under consideration as a potential vice-presidential pick. However, he ultimately chose Kamala Harris. In the 2020 election cycle, Georgia flipped from Republican to Democrat as Biden won the state—and the national election—and Jon Ossoff and Raphael Warnock were both victorious in their races, securing Democratic control of the U.S. Senate. Many credited Abrams with her party's success in Georgia.

Abrams wrote a number of books. Her nonfiction works include Minority Leader: How to Lead from the Outside and Make Real Change (2018; also published as Lead from the Outside: How to Build for Your Future and Make Real Change) and Our Time Is Now: Power, Purpose, and the Fight for a Fair America (2020). She also published the thriller While Justice Sleeps (2021) as well as several children's books.[xxiv]

Stuart Rojstaczer @stuarth2o

I am overeducated and like to tell jokes. I was raised in Milwaukee (my parents were Polish-Jewish immigrants) and have lived in Italy, Israel and everywhere in America except the Northeast. I have been a Duke University professor and a restaurant dishwasher (one paid a lot better, the other might have been a bit more fun). I am generally very happy and sometimes very cranky. I have been married for longer than is legal in California (shhh...do not tell the authorities). Somehow along the way, I became America's grade inflation czar (I do not understand how this happened, honest).

Congressional laws, Supreme Court briefs, and a presidential candidate's speeches (actually I was not too happy about that, but that is another story) have referenced my research. My work has been used to champion the launch of NASA earth observing satellites. It's all been unexpected and usually a kick. Plus, it gave my mom, when she was alive, reason to kvell, although grandchildren made her kvell more.

I've written tons of science articles, hundreds of songs, a good number of op-eds for newspapers, one opera (with composer William Susman) about Henry Ford, a few plays, and two books: one published memoir about my days as a professor (Gone for Good, Oxford, 1999) and a comic novel about Polish-Russian émigrés, The Mathematician's Shiva, which was published by Penguin Books in September 2014.

The novel is partly about the Navier-Stokes Millennium Prize problem, which examines the mathematical appropriateness of the Navier-Stokes equation to describe turbulent fluid flow. But mostly the novel is a comedy about the American immigrant experience.

I am currently putting the finishing touches on a new novel about an Omaha family that owns an Italian restaurant whose success depends on the fragile support of Omaha's most famous resident, Warren Buffett.[xxv]

Joanne L. Molinaro
@thekoreanvegan

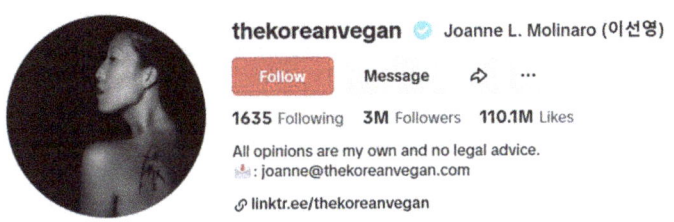

Molinaro is a Korean American woman, born in Chicago, Illinois. Her parents were both born in what is now known as North Korea. Molinaro started her blog, The Korean Vegan, in 2016, after adopting a plant-based diet. In July 2020, she started her TikTok (@thekoreanvegan), mostly as a coping mechanism for the isolation caused by the global pandemic. She began posting content related to politics and life as a lawyer during quarantine. However, after a single post of her making Korean braised potatoes for dinner (while her husband taught a piano lesson in the background) went viral, Molinaro shifted her attention to producing 60 second recipe videos, while telling stories about her family—immigrants from what is now known as North Korea.

With over 5 million fans spread across her social media platforms, New York Times best-selling author Joanne Molinaro, a.k.a The Korean

Vegan, has appeared on The Food Network, CBS Saturday Morning, ABC's Live with Kelly and Ryan, The Today Show, PBS, and The Rich Roll Podcast. She has been featured in the Los Angeles Times, The Washington Post, The Atlantic, NPR, and CNN; and her debut cookbook was selected as one of "The Best Cookbooks of 2021" by The New York Times and The New Yorker, among others.[xxvi]

JESSICA MCDONALD
@THE.LAUGHING.LAWY

the.laughing.lawy Jessica McDonald

Follow   Message

1138 Following   158.9K Followers   2.8M Likes

Recovering Republican, lawyer, mom
YouTube - @JessicaWarnerMcDonald

🔗 jessicamcdonald517888.subs...

An article published by Angela Johnson, on March 19, 2025, in The Root, titled: **"White Woman on TikTok Begs White Folks to Fight Trump's Segregation Push, But Black People's Response Will Surprise You... If You're White"** sheds lights on the video published by Jessica McDonald on TikTok, reporting the following:

As the Trump administration continues its "anti-woke" agenda, it recently announced that it would roll back a clause in the Federal Acquisition Regulation (which is used to write Federal contracts) that prohibits Federal contractors from having segregated restaurants, waiting rooms, and drinking fountains. The news should be shocking to everyone —except the 8 in 10 Black voters who came out in support of Vice President Kamala Harris in the 2024 Presidential election. Now, a white woman who acknowledges that Black people have more than done their part is calling on her fellow white people to get involved.

Jessica McDonald, known on TikTok as @the.laughing.lawy, posted a now-viral video explaining what is at stake as the Trump administration 2.0 attempts to roll back policies against segregation.

"It is no longer illegal to require separate facilities for people of different races," she said in her tear-filled post. "To be clear, the Civil Rights Act of 1964 is still in place. It has not been disbanded, but we know what their goal is."

McDonald, who mentioned in the comments of her post that she has two biracial daughters, went on to say that Black people have by and large led the fight against segregation while most white people have been sitting on the sidelines.

"Our Black countrymen have done their time at the front of the lines, and it is our turn. It is our turn to face the water hoses and to face the dogs and to face the tear gas, because we have let this happen," she said.

McDonald's post has received over 44,000 likes and thousands of comments from Black people who are more than happy to pass the torch to white folks.

"My mother marched alongside Medgar Evers. She was beaten, bitten by dogs, and dove under houses running from dogs and police. Yep. We have served our time. It is ya'll's now. Make America great please!" wrote someone in the comments.

Others flat out told McDonald that they plan to sit this fight out, opting to focus on self-care instead.

"I ain't marching. I am taking a nap," wrote another commenter.

But white people heard McDonald's cry for help, saying they understand what is at stake this time around.

"We are in a constitutional crisis!!!! We do not have much time left!!!" wrote someone.

We will be watching to see if McDonald can convince white folks to get up and get involved – from the couch, of course.[xxvii]

SCOT LOYD @THESCOTLOYD

Scot Loyd is a thoughtful speaker, writer, and teacher who digs into big questions about race, religion, and culture. Raised in rural Arkansas with deep roots in the Pentecostal faith, Scot blends his personal history with a critical look at today's social issues. With two master's degrees in communication and Heritage Studies, he brings both knowledge and heart to his work, whether he is teaching, sharing insights on social media, or speaking to audiences. Known for his clear thinking and relatable storytelling, Scot challenges people to see the world—and their beliefs—a little differently.[xxviii]

Justin @thewokeginger

thewokeginger thewokeginger

Follow   Message

51 Following   218.2K Followers   4.9M Likes

Just a 6"3 🏳️‍🌈 Ginger. In the clerb we all fam.
PayPal: thewokeginger

🔗 linktr.ee/thewokeginger

More links: https://linktr.ee/thewokeginger

MICHAEL MCWHORTER @TIZZYENT

Michael McWhorter (Born on June 11, 1976) is an American writer, director, and editor who specializes in TV music videos, feature films, and movie trailers. He currently works at Rhino Studios/Tizz Entertainment.

Michael, currently working as a writer, editor, and producer with L7 Pictures, has over 14 years of experience editing professionally. He has spent 8 years running a post at Rhino Studios in Miami, Florida, doing several duties, including writing, and recording voice-overs, color correction and color grading, and selecting and composing music as well as sound design.

Michael has written and directed several award-winning short films, ranking him among the best directors and writers in the world. One of his most notable projects is a short film, which he shot for under $100 and went on to win first place in the student category at the 2003 Palm Beach International Film Festival. In 2000, he formed his own production company, "Tizzy

Entertainment," which has released very highly rated films.[xxix]

Total Hipocrisy @TOTALHYPOCRISY

On her YouTube channel describes the channel: *"Exposing Double Standards 🕵 Truth > Propaganda."*

More links: https://bsky.app/profile/totalhypocrisy.bsky.social

Touré Neblett @toureshow

toureshow Toure YT: Rap Latte

9871 Following   486.1K Followers   11.4M Likes

YouTube.com/@raplatte
My Substack: Culture Fries
Vet of MTV, MSNBC, BET, CNN

🔗 toure.substack.com

My broadcast career has spanned major networks and cable outlets both as a host and contributor: I hosted The Cycle on MSNBC, Hip Hop Shop on Fuse, the Black Carpet on BET, I will Try Anything Once on Treasure HD, and Spoke N Heard on MTV. I was also the first Pop Culture correspondent on CNN.

A respected voice in the community, I consistently lend it to amplify causes for social justice and political awareness.

I write because it is the most natural thing in the world to me. I write because I love making sentences. I write because I like to talk about the world in ways that could challenge how people think. I write because I love talking about Black people and Black culture and the beauty of Blackness.

I have published six books including I Would Die 4 U: Why Prince Became an Icon and Who's Afraid of Post-Blackness: A Look at What It

Means to Be Black Now. I host the podcast Toure Show — guests have included Zadie Smith, Malcolm Gladwell, Ice Cube, Spike Lee, Kareem Abdul-Jabbar, Nikki Giovanni, Toni Braxton, Taraji P. Henson, and many others. I love using media to help challenge people's perception of themselves and of the world.

I love to talk about culture, politics, and the direction this country is going. I care deeply about America, pop culture, and my family—I have a wife, a son, and a daughter. I started out writing about music for Rolling Stone, as a Contributing Editor I did cover stories on Jay-Z, Beyonce, Lauryn Hill, Snoop Dogg, the Migos, Adele, and many others. I segued into TV as a pop culture correspondent for CNN, then hosted shows for MTV2, BET, and Fuse, then became the host of The Cycle on MSNBC.[xxx]

Roy Casagranda
@TRUE_STORY_GUY

I successfully defended my dissertation with the Department of Germanic Studies at the University of Texas at Austin on May Day 2017. I am proud to be a Longhorn and grateful to Katie Arens, PhD my dissertation chair and my committee for the opportunity.

I am Professor of Government at Austin Community College (ACC).

My research interests lie at the intersection of politics, history, economics, psychology, and philosophy. I am a firm believer in a multidisciplinary approach. Circa 1025 A.D. Ibn Sina (Avicenna) said, "The knowledge of anything, since all things have causes, is not acquired or complete unless it is known by its causes." It is my belief that understanding the causes of a thing, many approaches are necessary.

I have been a teacher since spring of 1995. I began teaching at college level in spring of 2002. There is nothing else that I would rather be doing.

I regularly give public lectures and news interviews. Since summer 2006 I have averaged around one public speaking event per month.

I am ACC's Middle East Affairs expert and have been doing television interviews since December 2008. As of late I have had the honor of doing several live interviews on KVUE (ABC) and Fox 7.

I am the founder and president of the Austin School, a student club and lecture series.

From September 2010 until early 2012 I wrote regularly for Merhnameh, a leading Tehran-based reformist socio-political monthly on US and Arab politics and history. I produced approximately one article every two to three months until the magazine was shut down by the Islamic Republic. I have also written one article for Hamshahri and another for Donya-e-Eqtesad Daily newspaper.

In the US I have written a piece for the Austin American Statesman as well as three articles for TODO Austin, each about the Arab Spring.

I wrote the University of Maryland University College's WWII classroom modules, and I have edited two of Jason Mark's books on WWII: Island of Fire and Besieged.

I am currently on the Faculty Evaluation Committee for the Department of Government at ACC.

I am 12/32 Egyptian, 6/32 Italian, 5/32 Finnish, 3/32 German, 3/32 Arab, and 3/32 Swedish. I have lived in both Germany and Egypt and speak German and Arabic. I have also lived in Lebanon, Algeria, and England and have traveled much of central and eastern Europe as well as some of the Middle East.

My personal interests include travel, backpacking, camping, gardening, and playing Advanced Squad Leader.[xxxi]

JOANNA JOHNSON @UNLEARN16

Sarcasm is my love language.

You have to learn — and often unlearn — in order to grow.

Ajax (Ontario, Canada) resident Joanna Johnson has taken to TikTok to help people do just that, and the response has been overwhelming.

"If I wasn't in teaching I never would have done it," Johnson said of TikTok, where 1.1 million people currently follow her account @unlearn16.

She started posting during lockdown as a way to connect in isolation. It began mostly with dance videos and lip-syncs, but one day Johnson decided to share her thoughts on current events and was surprised by the response.

"I started to talk a little bit more and give my opinion, first on silly things like which spoon to use to eat cereal or how to eat an Oreo, but then it started to get more political, and I had an incredible response," she recalls.

"That is when it sorts of clicked for me that 'oh, I can be myself and address the things that are important to me.' I try to be funny when I can, even though most of what is going on right now is not very funny and I try to be respectful in the way I address people, even people who send me hate."

That type of respectful discourse is a crucial element of Johnson's platform, and she has brought it with her to her new podcast, Unlearn16: Class is in Session.

"Every once in a while someone will come on my page and say something stupid, and I will just talk to them until some of them — not all of them — will say 'You know what, I'm sorry, I judged you'," she explains.

"That is the victory right there. People who already agree with me, I do not need to educate them, but to talk to people who come at me with hate or judgment, which is my true audience, because I think those conversations are vital. The only way we get to better solutions is by people who adamantly disagree still having intelligent, mindful, respectful discourse."

Johnson teaches full-time at a private secondary school in Toronto, and praises both school administration and students for supporting her extracurricular activities.

"I think it's a testament to the school I work at for encouraging that kind of thinking," she said.

"I get a lot of followers telling me 'I wish you could teach my kids' and that to me is the highest compliment. All the power of change comes from education and fighting for diversity and inclusivity. A lot of people keep their work life and private life separate but for me teaching is just who I am."

Johnson notes that she walks the walk as well, constantly learning — and unlearning — from her students, her girlfriend, her family and more.

"I'm very open to ways I have come up against it," said Johnson, who recalls a female student breaking down the inherent double standards in school dress codes for her about four years ago and how it opened her eyes.

"She was 1000 per cent right, and I never addressed an off the shoulder shirt again."

That willingness to learn and grow and change is at the heart of Johnson's TikTok podcast, and it is something she will continue to encourage as she embarks on a new string of speaking engagements.[xxxii]

The Author

Juan Ramon Rodulfo Moya, **Defined by Nature**: Inhabitant of Planet Earth, Human, Son of Eladio Rodulfo and Briceida Moya, Brother of Gabriela, Gustavo and Katiuska, Father of Gabriel and Sofia; **Defined by society**: Venezuelan Citizen (Limited Human Rights by default), Friend of many, enemy of few, Neighbor, Student/Teacher/Student, Worker/Supervisor/Manager/Leader/Worker, Husband of K/Ex-Husband of K/Husband of Y; **Defined by the U.S. Immigration Office**: Legal Alien; **Classroom studies**: Master's Degree in Human Resource Management, English, Mandarin Chinese; **Real-World Studies**: Human Behavior; **Home Studios**: SEO Webmaster, Graphic Design, Application and Website Development, Internet and Social Media Marketing, Video Production, YouTube Branding, Part 107 Commercial Drone Pilot, Import-Export, Affiliate Marketing, Cooking, Laundry, Home Cleaning; **Work experience**: Public-Private-Entrepreneurial Sectors; **Other definitions:** Bitcoin Evangelist, Defender of Human Rights, Peace and Love.

juanrodulfo.com

Publications:

Books:

- Why Maslow: How to use his theory to stay in Power Forever (EN/SP)
- Asylum Seekers (EN/SP)
- Manual for Gorillas: 9 Rules to be the "Ferpect" Dictator (EN/SP)
- Why you must Play the Lottery (EN/SP); Para Español Oprima #2: Speaking Spanish in Times of Xenophobia (EN/SP)
- Cause of Death: IGNORANCE | Human Behavior in Times of PANIC (EN/SP)
- Politics explained for Millennials, GENs XYZ and future generations (EN/SP)
- Las cenizas del Ejército Libertador (EN/SP)
- Remain Silent: The only right we have. The legal Aliens (EN/SP)
- Fortune Cookie Coaching 88 Motivational Tips Made Of Fortune Cookies, Vol I (EN)
- Vicky Erotic Tales, Vol I (EN)

Blogs:

Noticias de Nueva Esparta, Ubuntu Café, Coffee Secrets, Guaripete Pro, Rodulfox, Red Wasp Drone, Barista Pro, Gorila Travel, Fortune Cookie Coach, All Books, Vicky Toys.

juanrodulfo.com

Audiovisual Productions:
Podcasts:
Ubuntu Cafe | Vicky Erotic Tales | Fortune Cookie Coach | All Books, available at: juanrodulfo.com/podcasts

Music:
Albums: Margarita | Race to Extinction | Relaxed Panda | Amazonia | Cassiopeia | Caracas | Arcoiris Musical | Close Your Eyes, disponibles en: juanrodulfo.com/music

Photography & Video:
On sale at Adobe Stock, iStock, Shutterstock, and Veectezy, available at: juanrodulfo.com/gallery

Social Media Profiles:
Twitter / FB / Instagram / TikTok/ VK / LinkedIn / Sina Weibo: @rodulfox
Google Author: https://g.co/kgs/grjtN5
Google Artist: https://g.co/kgs/H7Fiqg
Twitter: https://twitter.com/rodulfox
Facebook: https://facebook.com/rodulfox
LinkedIn: https://www.linkedin.com/in/rodulfox
Instagram: https://www.instagram.com/rodulfox/
VK: https://vk.com/rodulfox
TikTok: https://www.tiktok.com/@rodulfox
Trading

View: https://www.tradingview.com/u/rodulfox/

Table of Contents

Preface 7
Aaron Gideon Parnas @aaronparnas1 13
ACLU @aclu 17
William Tong @agwilliamtong 25
Alberta Tech @alberta.nyc 29
@alimcforever 31
Alexandria Ocasio-Cortez @aoc 33
John Aravosis @aravosis 41
Ashley Thee Barroness @ashleytheebarroness 43
@atheisticdeist 45
Bernie Sanders @bernie 47
Brad Bernstein @bradbernsteinlaw 49
Stewart Reynolds @brittlestar 51
Captain Mark Kelly @captmarkkelly 53
Claudia Sheinbaum Pardo @claudiasheinbaum 57
Brandt Robinson @climberbrandt 61
Dannie D. @dannie01 65
Ash Dobrofsky @dashdobrofsky 67
David Pakman @davidpakmanshow 71
CDejavu @dejavu_candy 75

Eden @edensingsofficial 77
Facts to Grind @factstogrind 79
Hal_for_NY__ @hal_for_ny__ 81
Bootsy Sanders @he.cold3 83
Leigh McGowan @iampoliticsgirl 85
Isa Bako @isa_bako 91
Jared Van @jaredvaneducation 93
Jasmine Crockett @jasmineforus 95
Joy Ann Reid @joyreidofficial 99
Lisa Yahne @lisayay1966 103
Michael David Gantt @mdg650hawk7thacct
.... 105
MercurialLuvr @mercurialluvr 109
Mercedes Chandler @mercychandler 111
Reid Moon @moonsrarebooks 113
Neil deGrasse Tyson @neildegrassetyson 115
Jon_48 @openlyblack 125
Alex Pearlman @pearlmania500 127
PissedMagistus @pissedmagistus 129
PissedoffBartender @pissedoffbartender 131
Mike M @rationalboomer 133
Robert Reich @rbreich 135
Ro Khanna @reprokhanna 139

juanrodulfo.com

Robert Garcia @robertgarcia 141
Sir Addison Witt @siraddisonwitt 145
Stacey Abrams @staceyabrams 149
Stuart Rojstaczer @stuarth20 153
Joanne L. Molinaro @thekoreanvegan 155
Jessica McDonald @the.laughing.lawy 157
Scot Loyd @thescotloyd 161
Justin @thewokeginger 163
Michael McWhorter @tizzyent 165
Total Hipocrisy @totalhypocrisy 167
Touré Neblett @toureshow 169
Roy Casagranda @true_story_guy 171
Joanna Johnson @unlearn16 175
The Author 179
   Publications: 180
      Books: 180
      Blogs: 180
   Audiovisual Productions: 181
      Podcasts: 181
      Music: 181
      Photography & Video: 181
   Social Media Profiles: 181
Notes 187

Notes

i DPA/The Local, Ever more people worldwide living under dictatorship, German study finds, 22 March 2018 10:15 CET+01:00, fetched from: https://www.thelocal.de/20180322/ever-more-people-worldwide-living-under-dictatorship-german-study-finds

ii Wikipedia, Aaron Parnas, available at: https://en.wikipedia.org/wiki/Aaron_Parnas, visited on March 18, 2025

iii ACLU, American Civil Liberties Union, available at: https://www.aclu.org/, Visited on March 18, 2025

iv Office of the Attorney General State of Connecticut, Attorney general William Tong Biography, available at: https://portal.ct.gov/ag/about-the-ag/william-tong-biography-page, visited on March 18, 2025

v Alexandria Ocasio-Cortez, About, available at: https://ocasio-cortez.house.gov/about, visited on March 18, 2025

vi Bernie Sanders, About, available at: https://www.sanders.senate.gov/about-bernie/, visited on March 18, 2025

vii Wikipedia, Brittlestar, available at: https://en.wikipedia.org/wiki/Brittlestar, visited on March 18, 2025

viii Britannica, Mark Kelly, available at: https://www.britannica.com/topic/NASA, visited on March 18, 2025

ix Britannica, Claudia Sheinbaum, available at: https://www.britannica.com/biography/Claudia-Sheinbaum, visited on March 18, 2025

x FEA, Pinellas teacher and activist honored by FEA, available at: https://feaweb.org/release/pinellas-teacher-and-activist-honored-by-fea/, visited on March 26, 2025

[xi] Famous People FAQ Bilali, Who Is Dash Dobrofsky? All You Need To Know About Him, available at: https://famouspeoplefaq.com/dash-dobrofsky/, visited on March 26, 2025

[xii] Wikipedia, David Pakman, available at: https://en.wikipedia.org/wiki/David_Pakman, visited on March 26, 2025

[xiii] Politicsgirl, ABOUT POLITICSGIRL, available at: https://www.politicsgirl.com/about, visited on March 26, 2025

[xiv] Van Jared, More About me, available at: https://www.jaredvan.com/about-me, visited on March 26, 2025

[xv] House.gov, About the congresswoman, available at: https://crockett.house.gov/about, visited on March 26, 2025

[xvi] Wikipedia, Joy Reid, available at: https://en.wikipedia.org/wiki/Joy_Reid, visited on March 26, 2025

[xvii] GB Times, Who is mdg650hawk TikTok real name?, available at: https://gbtimes.com/who-is-mdg650hawk-tiktok-real-name/, visited on March 26, 2025

[xviii] Moons Rare Books, About, available at: https://moons-rare-books.myshopify.com/pages/about, visited on March 28, 2025

[xix] Wikipedia, Neil deGrasse Tyson, available at: https://en.wikipedia.org/wiki/Neil_deGrasse_Tyson, visited on March 28, 2025

[xx] Wikipedia, Robert Reich, available at: https://en.wikipedia.org/wiki/Robert_Reich, visited on March 28, 2025

[xxi] House.gov, Congressman Ro Khanna, available at: https://khanna.house.gov/about, visited on March 28, 2025

[xxii] House.gov, Congressman Robert Garcia, available at: https://robertgarcia.house.gov/about, visited on March 28, 2025
[xxiii] Adisson Witt, About Me, available at: https://www.siraddisonwitt.com/about-me, visited on March 28, 2025
[xxiv] Britannica, Stacey Abrams, available at: https://www.britannica.com/biography/Stacey-Abrams, visited on: March 28, 2025
[xxv] Stuart Rojstaczer, About Me, available at: https://stuartr.com/about-me/, visited on March 28, 2025
[xxvi] Joanne Lee Molinaro, About, available at: https://thekoreanvegan.com/about/, visited on March 28, 2025
[xxvii] Angela Johnson, The Root, White Woman on TikTok Begs White Folks to Fight Trump's Segregation Push, But Black People's Response Will Surprise You... If You're White, March 19, 2025, available at: https://www.theroot.com/white-woman-on-tiktok-begs-white-folks-to-fight-against-1851770972, visited on March 28, 2025
[xxviii] Scotloyd.com, Author: scotloyd, available at: https://scotloyd.com/author/scotloyd/, visited on March 28, 2025
[xxix] Famous People FAQ, Michael McWhorter, available at: https://famouspeoplefaq.com/michael-mcwhorter/, visited on March 28, 2025
[xxx] Toure.com, Touré, available at: https://toure.com, visited on March 28, 2025
[xxxi] Austin Community College, Roy Casagranda, available at: https://gov.casagranda.com/about/index.html, visited on March 28, 2025
[xxxii] Unlearn16, About, available at: https://unlearn16.com/about-me, visited on March 28, 2025

www.ingramcontent.com/pod-product-compliance
Lightning Source LLC
LaVergne TN
LVHW052245070526
838201LV00113B/346/J